Oral
History

From Tape to Type

Oral History

From Tape to Type

Cullom Davis
Kathryn Back
Kay MacLean

Chicago

American Library Association

1977

Library of Congress Cataloging in Publication Data

Davis, Cullom, 1935-
    Oral history.

    Bibliography: p.
    1.   Oral history.   2.   Libraries—Special collections
—Oral history.   I.   Back, Kathryn, 1946-   joint
author.   II.   MacLean, Kay, 1939-   joint author.
III.   Title.
D16.14.D38   907   77-4403
ISBN 0-8389-0230-8 pbk.   *Ap 578*

Printed in the United States of America

Contents

Figures

Preface

This book was conceived and designed as a guide for the small or beginning oral history program, and as a textbook for oral history instruction. It is both an instructional and operating manual in that careful readers can learn all of the basic oral history steps from it. It is also a workbook because various illustrations and exercises have been included to enable the novice to perfom and practice certain skills. Throughout the text there are sample forms indicating how to do the paperwork that accompanies oral history interviewing and processing. These forms may be revised or adapted to suit particular programs. There is an appendix of useful reference information, including a glossary and rules of style for editing.

While the book is thus suitable for self-instruction, readers should understand that oral history cannot be learned, let alone mastered, solely through independent study. Careful instruction and supervision by experienced persons are also necessary, particularly in the area of interviewing technique. Moreover, each step in oral history requires much more practice than the simple exercises herein provide. Learners should rehearse their technique repeatedly and arrange for personal consultation and review on every step. With this caveat in mind readers may follow the various steps and exercises progressively, and also may find this book useful as a reference work for subsequent questions and problems.

Another important feature in the pages that follow is an emphasis on disseminating the oral history product to students, researchers, and the interested public. Oral history's remarkable growth in recent years has understandably but unfortunately concentrated on collecting and processing. Practitioners have given insufficient attention to methods for retrieving, publishing, and publicizing their work. As oral history programs enter a period of more orderly growth they must face the task of dissemination, and this book attempts to offer guidance and suggestions.

The authors wrote an early draft of this book for an oral history workshop sponsored by the Illinois State Library in 1975. We drew upon several years of personal and collaborative experience in managing the Oral History Office at Sangamon State University and building its collection of tapes and transcripts. We received valuable criticism and assistance from Syma Mendelsohn, Harold Kipp, Barbara Scheibling, Sheila Sears, Rosalyn Bone, and Sue Williamson of Sangamon State University.

I

Understanding Oral History

In recent years the recording of conversations on tape has attracted increasing public attention, both favorable and unfavorable. On the bright side have been popular films, radio programs, and bestselling books based on the oral history premise; the spread of oral history instruction on college campuses and within local historical groups; and the dramatic growth of oral history programs, which now number thousands of practitioners, tens of thousands of hours of recorded interviews, and millions of pages of transcript. This oral history boom has been countered by public revulsion against the notorious misuse of tape recorders for ulterior and subversive purposes that threaten individual privacy and civil liberties.

The Old and the New

Putting aside all the excitement of bestselling books and/or political scandals, oral history is nothing more than a branch of historical research. In that context it is the offspring of history's most ancient technique and its most modern technology. Its technique is the collection of eyewitness accounts to history; the ancient Greek historians did this more than two thousand years ago. Its technology, the compact tape recorder, is as modern as the space age.

This paradoxical marriage of the old and the new is generally credited to the celebrated historian Allan Nevins, who in 1948 founded an oral history program at Columbia University. Since then the movement has mushroomed, with hundreds of oral history programs underway in every state and around the world. Columbia's Oral History Research Office still leads the field, however, followed by major programs in selected universities and at presidential libraries.

1

People's History

Initially oral history was promoted as a means of supplementing the voluminous written record of celebrities and other important persons. This elitist focus has shifted radically in recent years; many newer programs deliberately concentrate on interviewing common people. This is due first to the rapid growth of the movement; today there probably are more oral historians than there are dignitaries to interview. Thus oral history's version of the law of supply and demand has prompted interviewers to liberalize their criteria for selecting narrators. A second reason for the focal change is the general trend throughout the historical profession toward "people's history," as scholars display a heightened interest in the lives of factory hands, migrant workers, and ghetto dwellers. Finally, oral historians have come to recognize that they have more to contribute by interviewing common people than by talking to celebrities.

At best oral history will only modestly supplement the massive written record concerning most famous people, but it often represents all we can learn about the lives of ordinary persons. Coal miners and country schoolteachers rarely document their lives with letters or diaries, and their only recognition in newspapers is likely to be the vital statistics of their birth, marriage, and death. In a relative sense, then, oral history offers immensely more to the subject of social and folk history than it does to our knowledge of the American presidency or diplomatic history. This egalitarian bent is a conspicuous feature of the oral history movement today, though many established programs continue their emphasis on leaders and elites.

Local History

A related trend has been oral history's application to the study of local and regional history. As interest has shifted from celebrities to common people, so has the focus moved from the national or international setting to state and local history. This, too, can partly be explained by the grass roots movement underway in the historical profession, and by the higher potential oral history has for influencing the more limited scope and subject matter of local history. Rarely can an oral history interview directly affect our knowledge and interpretation of American history, but in state and local history it often is decisive and sometimes is the only historical data available.

Another reason for the growing emphasis on local history is oral history's popularity among amateur historians whose research interests and capabilities are limited to their home towns. Thousands of citizen-historians have been drawn to oral history because of its novelty, popularity, and apparent simplicity. Their interest in discovering and preserving the past through interviewing, coupled with their typical preference for "backyard history," has tied another knot in the close relationship between the practice of oral history and the subject matter of local history. One measure of this partnership is the fact that the nation's largest and best-known sponsor of local history study—the American Association for State and Local History—is the publisher of two manuals on oral history technique.

What are the implications and pitfalls of oral history's growing affinity with both people's history and local history? First it must be recognized that the relationship is a natural and mutually beneficial one. The interviewing technique serves the grass roots history movement well, and in turn it has prospered as the latter's methodological companion.

Second, oral history has performed an important service in providing access to the folk history of groups whose heritage might otherwise be lost. This is particularly true of groups and cultures that for some reason have a predominantly oral rather than written tradition. The oral history medium has unlocked and preserved the folk history of American blacks and Indian groups, thereby beginning in a small way to compensate for the paucity of accurate documents or other printed matter.

Third, the spoken reminiscences of common people have helped historians rediscover and more effectively use folk history. Without detracting from the significance of presidents and other agents of historical action we have come to appreciate the less fateful but nevertheless important role played by the objects of that action.

There are dangers in this, however. One is the tempting assumption that oral history can tell the whole story or even most of it. Local historical groups and volunteers must guard against permitting their enthusiasm for oral history to neglect other historical sources, such as newspapers, diaries, photographs, and manuscript collections. Zealots of the tape-recorder approach have been known to waste much time and money interviewing persons without bothering to discover that the entire story is already available in some documentary form. As a research technique oral history can and should never be regarded as more than one modestly useful way of gaining access to a distinctive but fallible historical source, the human memory.

Another danger is oral history's susceptibility to collecting trivial information. The untutored interviewer who lacks historical perspective easily succumbs to filling tape with personal information that carries little if any historical value. A thirty-minute exchange on the subject of family motor trips is unlikely to yield insights or generalizations about American social history. The skilled interviewer will steer toward subject matter that can help build themes and patterns of folk history.

Other Paradoxes

Oral history has other paradoxes besides ancient technique and advanced technology. Its mode is as elementary as human conversation but also as complex as the fields of audio engineering, electronics, and information retrieval combined. It can be as economical as a $2-reel of recording tape or as expensive in processing costs as $250 for every hour of interview. Interviews may require only hours or even minutes to conduct, but it may take years to convert that tape into a bound typescript. Oral history deserves substantial credit for some prizewinning books in recent years, but it must also shoulder a measure of responsibility for adding both trivia and error to the world's storehouse of historical data. At its best it demonstrates ethical standards that warrant envy from the historical and library professions; at its worst, as in the case of the secret White House recording operation of several years ago, it exhibits frightening potential for violating personal privacy. As a fashionable and fast-growing enterprise it has its share of incompetents and charlatans as well as conscientious practitioners. It is an activity that draws upon the most sophisticated skills of professional historians but also can be undertaken productively by weekend amateurs.

Taping and Typing

As a branch of historical research, oral history logically divides into (1) the *collection* of data, (2) its *processing* into printed form, and (3) its *dissemination and use*. Viewed in the sense of both input and output, it follows a natural progression from the preliminary contacts and research to the final typing and cataloging. From the practicing historian's standpoint, there is little use or justification in simply collecting without disseminating. A case can be made, however, for those persons and institutions that suffer budget and personnel limitations to engage solely in collecting oral history interviews. There are two reasons for this. First, oral history represents the preservation of otherwise perishable historical data. Its raw material is the human memory, which of course survives only as long as its possessor lives, and often deteriorates even sooner. Merely preserving this fragile historical commodity can be a worthwhile endeavor. Second, there is always the opportunity for dissemination once the job of collecting and preserving has been done.

But it remains a fact that individuals and organizations that concentrate exclusively on collection and preservation of oral history are unlikely to enjoy the satisfaction of having their labors used or appreciated by the scholarly guild and the general public. Notwithstanding the proclamations of Marshall McLuhan and other prophets of the electronic era, we continue to live in the age of the printed word, which means that raw oral history tapes will gather dust. At Columbia University's Oral History Research Office, patron requests for transcripts reportedly exceed those for tapes by a ratio of one thousand to one. The serious oral historian must confront this stark fact and sooner or later assume the burden of transcribing.

The Treadmill of Passing Time

Oral historians are haunted by the obituary page. Every death represents the loss of a potential narrator and thus an absolute diminution of society's collective historical memory. The veteran interviewer comes to accept this, but never altogether escapes remorse for failing to interview someone "while there was still time." Oral history's one weapon in this losing battle with time is its distinctive sequence of steps. It is unique among historical research techniques in that its first step—interviewing on tape—is also its most important and urgent step. Without a taped interview one has nothing; with it the collecting job is basically finished. From then on every successive stage of processing will enhance prospects for wider dissemination. Thus rough transcripts are an improvement over raw tapes and, in turn, edited transcripts are an improvement over the rough version. Each step in the complex and time-consuming business of processing is an improvement and an aid to greater public use. For some organizations with limited budgets and some interviews of marginal value, the law of diminishing returns may intervene at some point and argue against any further processing. A thoughtfully organized activity will be able to make the best of this state of affairs and offer its unfinished memoirs to an interested public in some usable form.

Oral History or Hearsay?

An obvious consequence of oral history's exclusive reliance upon the memories of living persons is that its scope is limited to those life spans. For practical purposes, therefore, its contribution is largely confined to our historical knowledge of the twentieth century. Anything a narrator reports about the lives of ancestors or the events of their times is oral hearsay, not oral history. This is not to say that such material is worthless but to face a fact about its veracity, to acknowledge that it is not an eyewitness account, and that it is thus not oral history.

Oral History or Heresy?

Of what value as authentic and credible historical data are an elderly person's recollections of the distant past? Oral history has been challenged and dismissed frequently on this point. True, human memory is a fragile historical source; it is subject to lapses, errors, fabrications, and distortions. Anyone who uncritically accepts an oral history memoir as historical truth is destined to misunderstand the past. The hundreds of thousands of transcript pages that constitute this nation's oral history storehouse contain a generous share of trivia, errors, and lies. But to acknowledge this sobering condition is not to deny the value of oral history. It is well to remember that:

1. All primary historical sources are subject to factual error, so in at least an absolute sense oral history is no less reliable than newspapers, personal correspondence, and presidential messages. The conscientious researcher adopts a skeptical view toward all data, including oral history.

2. Oral history makes no claim of exclusivity. On the contrary, practitioners view their work as supplementing and enriching the written record. In cases where a taped memoir is the only source available, as with many interviews of ordinary persons, oral historians acknowledge that the record is necessarily incomplete.

3. Proficient interviewers often can steer a narrator closer to the truth by approaching the same topic from several lines of inquiry.

4. Many oral history projects involve dozens of narrators recounting the same event or experience. By sifting these different versions, a researcher can often reconstruct the past in a way that will survive the standard tests of historical evidence.

5. Whatever its errors, an oral history memoir remains the closest thing to pure, unadulterated human memory. How someone recalls the past can provide revealing insights even if the story is of doubtful veracity. In such instances, the memoir becomes another kind of historical source that sophisticated researchers can put to good use.

6. Finally, there are instances in which oral history has proven more reliable and accurate than standard printed or manuscript sources. During a trial involving prosecution of Indians who had occupied Wounded Knee, South Dakota, expert witnesses argued effectively that Indian recollections of their sovereignty over that land were more credible than government documents claiming jurisdiction. Human memory, fragile and biased as it can be, can also be an extraordinary faculty.

Oral history, then, is not heresy. When conscientiously gathered, carefully processed, and critically examined, it contributes modestly to the quantity and uniquely to the quality of what we know about the recent past.

EXERCISE 1: THE USES OF ORAL HISTORY

A. Select one of the following books for an analysis of the published use of oral history interviews:

Bullock, Paul, ed. *Watts: The Aftermath; An Inside View of the Ghetto, by the People of Watts.* New York: Grove, 1969.

Burns, James MacGregor. *Roosevelt: The Soldier of Freedom.* New York: Harcourt, 1970.

Frankfurter, Felix. *Felix Frankfurter Reminisces, Recorded Talks with Harlan B. Phillips.* New York: Reynal, 1960.

Joseph, Peter. *Good Times: An Oral History of America in the Nineteen Sixties.* New York: Charterhouse, 1973.

Lash, Joseph P. *Eleanor and Franklin.* New York: Norton, 1971.

Miller, Merle. *Plain Speaking: An Oral Biography of Harry S. Truman.* New York: Putnam, 1974.

Montell, William L. *The Saga of Coe Ridge: A Study in Oral History.* Knoxville: Univ. of Tennessee Pr., 1970.

Rosengarten, Theodore. *All God's Dangers: The Life of Nate Shaw.* New York: Knopf, 1974.

Terkel, Studs. *Hard Times: An Oral History of the Great Depression in America.* New York: Pantheon, 1970.

Wigginton, Eliot, ed. *The Foxfire Book.* New York: Doubleday, 1972.

Williams, T. Harry. *Huey Long.* New York: Knopf, 1969.

B. Answer the following questions:

1. What approximate proportion of the total information in the book was from oral history sources?

2. Describe the form in which the oral history material is presented in the book (for example, "substantial excerpts included," "short comments quoted," "an entire memoir intact").

3. Does the author say or imply anything about oral history in comparison with other kinds of historical research and data? If so, what is the author's assessment?

4. In a qualitative sense what does the oral history material contribute to the book (for example, "illustrative anecdotes only," "chiefly descriptions of other persons")?

II

Collecting Oral History

T
he best-known and most glamorous phase of oral history is collecting and preserving tape-recorded interviews. In the public mind this is probably regarded as the totality of oral history, though in reality the interviewing constitutes only the first two steps in a complex eight-step process. These first steps are the most glamorous because they entail meeting all kinds of interesting people, involve the handling of electronic equipment, and give the practitioner a sense of unearthing new, and perhaps unique, historical information.

However, the excitement and appeal of this phase should not disguise its heavy demands and exacting standards. Collecting oral history requires proficiency in such specialized skills as historical research, equipment operation, and interviewing; it also demands sensitivity, alertness, and empathy on the part of the interviewers. Contrary to popular impression, preparation and interviewing can be tedious and tiring work, and sometimes even be unproductive. Veteran oral historians have had their share of unsuccessful projects, and a bad interview will always remain a bad interview.

Of some consolation (as well as anxiety) is the fact that collecting, if not the totality, is the *sine qua non* of oral history. Without a taped interview one can never have a transcript or a bound oral history memoir. Collecting is the crucial first stage of oral history and therefore it deserves careful attention and extensive practice by the novice.

The following pages are a guide through the various preliminaries and offer instruction in interviewing.

Step 1: Getting Ready

Careful planning and preparation are key elements in successful oral history interviewing. In most forms of research one can reexamine sources to correct a mistake or fill a gap, but with oral history there is ordinarily only one opportunity. Few narrators have the patience to cover the same ground due to faulty preparation or negligence by an interviewer. Since the oral historian depends on the goodwill and cooperation of narrators, it is imperative that he/she be well prepared for the initial and all subsequent sessions. Certain basic preliminaries are common to all interviews.

Selecting the Subject

Oral history comes in various forms. The most common is a simple *biographical* project in which the objective is to gather as much information about a narrator's life as possible. This is likely to be an extensive personal memoir, running for many taping sessions and resulting in a transcript of several hundred pages. The biographical memoir stands by itself as a singular contribution to history.

Sometimes oral historicans select a *topic* rather than one person for their subject. In this case one will interview many persons about the topic, possibly limiting the interview in each case to a particular episode. (An example would be a project on mayors or Italian Americans in a community.) One disadvantage of this thematic approach is the likelihood that interviews will be one-dimensional rather than comprehensive.

Similar to the above is the project that points to a particular historical *event* by interviewing some of its participants or observers. For example, a person might select a project on the home front in his or her community during World War II.

Most oral history programs pursue each of these approaches. The important thing is to choose the projects carefully according to the distinctive needs, resources, and opportunities of one's program.

Selecting the Narrator

Develop a card file of prospective narrators. Start the file by asking friends, neighbors, and colleagues for suggestions; addressing civic and other local group meetings; approaching elderly citizen associations, such as retired teachers; and contacting nursing homes. Once the interviewing activities become generally known in the community, you will probably receive a steady flow of unsolicited nominations to add to the card file. It does not take long for a prospects file to grow into a frustrating backlist. The file should contain such information as the name, address, and telephone number of the prospect; the name and relationship (if any) of the person suggesting this prospect; plus available information or assumptions on the likely subject and scope of an interview (see figure 1).

> Gordon, Eleanor (Mrs. Harold)
> 1427 E. Washington Street
> Danville   763-4218
> recommended by James Stryker (nephew)
> _____
> Prospect reportedly has a vivid memory &
> a willingness to discuss her career as a
> pioneer social worker in Kankakee, plus
> general recollections
>   CD 2/12/74

Fig. 1. A prepared file card for a prospective narrator.

Select a prospective narrator according to the program's priorities as well as your own sense of his/her potential as a subject. In some cases interviewers pay heed to the actuarial tables and contact their oldest prospects first. A more typical approach is to select a particular theme or topic (for example, "Elm-town during the Great Depression") and to contact persons who reportedly can contribute valuable recollections.

While it is dangerous to base selection too heavily on preliminary pro and con impressions of a candidate's potential, there are several personal criteria to consider. One is the tentative estimate of his/her memory; is it extensive, detailed, and reliable? Also, does the prospect appear to be interested in the past? To put it another way, does the prospect enjoy talking about old times? Another criterion is the individual's self-confidence and sense of personal worth. Anyone who belittles his/her own lifetime and career is not likely to be a good prospect for oral history.

Valuable narrators come from all walks of life, occupations, and backgrounds. Often the best ones, however, have held some job or occupied themselves in some way that made them attentive observers of the passing scene. Bartenders, policemen, cab drivers, reporters, mailmen, and active citizens ordinarily fall in this category, but beware of excluding others whose attentiveness is the product of personal nature rather than occupation.

Initial Contact

Telephone or write the prospect, informing him/her of your work and interest in interviewing. If the prospect consents, gather basic biographical information to assist with preliminary research, inform him/her fully about all legal and ethical matters, and schedule an exploratory, get-acquainted meeting.

Maintain written notes or a log (see figure 2) of all contacts with the narrator, and keep copies of all correspondence. This is also a good time to fill out the biographical data section of an INTERVIEW DATA SHEET as shown in figure 3. The entire top section should be completed before it and the tapes are eventually turned over to the oral history office.

The Preliminary Meeting

Establishing a good working relationship with the narrator will nourish trust and enthusiasm for the venture. The preliminary meeting should explore all of the possible areas of inquiry. You also may want to display the equipment which will be used, as well as a sample transcript. Reassure the narrator at this and subsequent sessions that oral history interviews are deliberately informal and conversational, and that he/she should not anticipate taping as one might look forward nervously to a radio broadcast or television appearance. Ask to borrow personal materials (scrapbooks, photograph albums, newspaper clippings, diaries, personal mementos) that can aid in the background research. A word of caution: it is disturbingly easy for this preliminary meeting to turn into a premature, unrecorded interview. Prevent this by keeping the appointment brief and asking the narrator to postpone reminiscences until the next meeting.

The Legal Release

This first meeting is the ideal time to obtain the narrator's signature on a legal release assigning literary and property rights of the tape and transcript to the sponsoring institution. Without a signed release, it is not safe to make the fruits of one's interviewing labor available to researchers, because one does not have the legal right to share another person's recollections.

Most desirable is an unconditional release, but some narrators may insist on imposing certain restrictions on the use of their recollections. One common form of restriction is to stipulate that a memoir may not be cited or quoted without permission from the narrator or his/her heirs. Another is to keep the memoir closed for a period of time, often five years or until the narrator's death (see figures 4 and 5).

Occasionally a narrator will balk, expressing distrust of the legal language in the release or suspicion of profitmaking motives on the interviewer's part. With patience and a trusting relationship one can usually overcome these fears. Point out that future generations will appreciate learning about the narrator's life. Also note that the prospects for commercial use of an oral history memoir are remote, and that actually the history office will be spending rather than making money on the project (the estimated cost of processing is eight dollars per page of completed typescript or two hundred dollars per hour of inter-

Contact Notes -- Eleanor Gordon

5/16/74 Checked with James Stryker (nephew) by phone about subject's general health and likely reaction to an interview. He reassured on both counts.

6/3/74 Wrote subject standard letter (see file)

6/8/74 ~~Telephoning~~ Telephoned subject as follow-up to letter; explained our program and arranged preliminary appointment. Also described legal release.

6/20/74 Appointment at subject's home. Reviewed plans and demonstrated tape recorder. Explained the legal release and secured her signature. Obtained biographical info for Interview Data Sheet. Looked through some photographs and letters; secured permission to have copies made. Scheduled first interview session.

Fig. 2. Sample contact notes.

Tri-County Historical Society
INTERVIEW DATA SHEET

This section is to be completed by the Interviewer.

NARRATOR _Harold Johnson_　ADDRESS _1127 38th Street, Indianapolis, Indiana_ PHONE _643-8812_

BIRTHDATE _4/12/08_　BIRTHPLACE _Brackington, Tennessee_ INTERVIEWER _Jane Rogers_　PHONE _342-4461_

DATE(S) & PLACE OF INTERVIEW(S) _7/14/75 7/20 7/24 8/3 Narrator's home_

COLLATERAL MATERIAL Yes [✓] No [ ]　TERMS _Open_

- -

This section is for office use. Write the date in the larger columns and check the smaller ones to record each process.

TAPES	Received & Labeled	Collaterals Filed	Transcribing			Catalogued	Audited	Editing		Review		Returned	Reread	Preface	Final Typing		Text Finished Index, Table of Contents	Proofread	Corrected	Duplicating						Distribution			Dissemination		
			Begun	No. of Pages	Total Time			Begun	Total Time	To Narrator					Begun					Transcript Sent	Transcript Returned	Tape Sent	Tape Returned	Shelf Copy	Narrator's Copy	NUOMC	Microfilm	Radio			

Fig. 3. Sample Interview Data Sheet.

Tri-County Historical Society

    For and in consideration of the participation by *Tri-County Historical Society* in any programs involving the dissemination of tape-recorded memoirs and oral history material for publication, copyright, and other uses, I hereby release all right, title, or interest in and to all of my tape-recorded memoirs to *Tri-County Historical Society* and declare that they may be used without any restriction whatsoever and may be copyrighted and published by the said *Society*, which may also assign said copyright and publication rights to serious research scholars.

    In addition to the rights and authority given to you under the preceeding paragraph, I hereby authorize you to edit, publish, sell and/or license the use of my oral history memoir in any other manner which the *Society* considers to be desirable and I waive any claim to any payments which may be received as a consequence thereof by the *Society*.

PLACE *Indianapolis, Indiana*

DATE *July 14, 1975*

Harold S. Johnson
(Interviewee)

Jane Rogers
(for *Tri-County Historical Society*)

Fig. 4. Sample unconditional release.

Tri-County Historical Society

I hereby release all right, title, or interest in and to all or any part of my tape-recorded memoirs to *Tri-County Historical Society*, subject to the following stipulations:

That my memoirs are to be closed until five years following my death.

PLACE *Indianapolis, Indiana*

DATE *July 14, 1975*

Harold S. Johnson
(INTERVIEWEE)

Jane Rogers
(for *Tri-County Historical Society*)

Fig. 5. Sample conditional release.

view). Finally, point out that the narrator will have an opportunity to review and correct the transcript before it is ready for final printing and public use.

Research

Before interviewing one should learn as much as possible about the narrator's life experiences and also the history of the period, community, profession, and so on, to be covered. The magnitude of such background research varies widely, depending on the amount of available data. Oral histories with famous persons can require months and even years of research into manuscript collections, public documents, newspapers, writings, and other conventional historical sources. With ordinary citizens there often is very little material to cover. Even in the latter case, however, one should become familiar with the history of the narrator's home town, occupation, and social milieu. Such knowledge will be indispensable in formulating precise questions like, "How did you react to the rumored failure of the Elmtown State Bank in 1932?" The personal scrapbooks and other memorabilia that you borrowed will be very useful for this phase of the preliminaries. Local libraries and historical society collections can also provide helpful information. One warning: in the course of research preparation, avoid the temptation to conceive of yourself as such an expert that you tend to second-guess the narrator or pose leading questions. Use the information acquired to ask open, not closed, questions.

The Interview Outline

With the research and other preparations completed, it is time to draft an outline of the subjects to be covered. A sample outline is shown in figure 6. Avoid the temptation to do this in a precise format which might result in stiff, formal questions and therefore create an unnatural interviewing atmosphere. This also might close your mind to fresh questioning avenues that invariably arise in the course of every interview. It is a good idea to send the narrator a copy of the outline in advance of the first interview, so that he/she will be prepared for its scope.

Final Preparations

Repeatedly practice with the recording equipment until you can operate it properly almost by instinct. This is vitally important in order to avoid unsettling the narrator with any signs of incompetence, to enable you to concentrate on the myriad other tasks involved in interviewing, and to minimize the risk of damaging a tape recording.

Check to make certain that the recorder and microphone are in proper working order. It is best to rely on electrical current for all interviewing, but if batteries must be used, make sure that they are fresh. Bring several spare tapes to each recording session. Pack an extension cord so that you will be free to interview in a comfortable and suitable place. Take at least two pens, the INTERVIEWER'S NOTES AND WORD LIST (see figure 7), any personal mementos you may have borrowed, and the copy of the interview outline.

Step 2: Interviewing

Effective oral history interviewing is a skill that some people possess naturally, others must acquire, and still others seem incapable of learning. The proficient oral historian employs interviewing methods that are not unique to his/her craft but are common to such other fields as journalism and communications, anthropology and folklore. The only difference is subject matter, not technique. Moreover, that technique is basic to human discourse; it is the

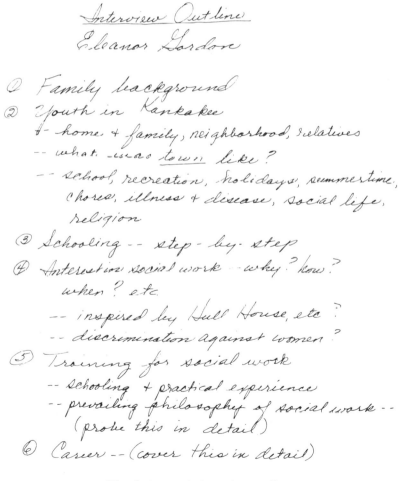

Fig. 6. A sample interview outline.

Tri-County Historical Society

INTERVIEWER'S NOTES AND WORD LIST

Instructions to the Interviewer:

To assist the transcriptionist, please identify:

1.   Passages which may be difficult to understand because of outside
     noise, other people in the room, problems with the tape recorder,
     and so forth.
2.   Passages which are confidential and therefore should not be typed.
3.   Passages which need to be treated in a special way.

Please list words or phrases which might be difficult to understand, all
proper names, and unfamiliar terms. If there is more than one tape, note
where the second and succeeding ones begin.

TAPE NO. _1_ Harold Johnson Interview (7/14/75)

Brockington, Tennessee
Gertrude ~~Fairley~~ Fairlie
Emmet Johnson
Aunt Edna (Johnson)
Indianapolis
Marion County
Fletcher Bank and Trust Company
Correspondent banking
"Bank Holiday" of 1933
<u>Note</u>: delete reference to employer's embezzlement,
beginning with "There was one incident. . . ." and
ending with "Maybe I shouldn't be talking
about that."
Lend Lease
Fort Leonard Wood
~~Calay~~ Calais
(Continue on Reverse)

Fig. 7. Interviewer's Notes and Word List.

conversation of a curious, attentive, and empathic listener. That is why the best oral historians have a natural and uncomplicated interviewing style. They exhibit interest in the subject, they are patient, they listen carefully and thoughtfully, and they formulate questions that are concise, simple, and straightforward.

Since not everyone possesses a natural gift for the craft there are some precepts and guidelines that can help the novice develop a good interviewing style. It is important to understand that the sole objective is to elicit informaion from the narrator, not to correct, debate, or educate. Ideally one should strive to create an atmosphere in which the narrator feels comfortable stretching his/her memory. That is why it is important to establish a personal relationship in advance of the first interviewing session. Engage in small talk before attempting to probe a person's life. This preliminary preparation allows a good opportunity for gathering basic biographical information for the INTERVIEW DATA SHEET shown in figure 3.

One Person at a Time

Sometimes it is tempting or almost unavoidable to interview more than one person. A spouse may be sitting in and occasionally interrupt with a comment or correction. While such additional information might be useful, the practice of having multiple narrators is at best dangerous and at worst disastrous. The interviewer is likely to lose control over what is happening and also miss opportunities to probe or pursue passing references. Moreover, the transcriptionist will have a very difficult time and the final product may more closely resemble a family argument than a personal memoir. Ask companions to sit quietly if they must be present; their turn may come later.

The Setting

A narrator is likely to feel most comfortable in familiar surroundings, such as a home or office. This is the ideal interviewing location provided such distractions as telephone interruptions and intrusions by a third party can be eliminated or at least minimized. One popular arrangement is to sit at a desk or table which is comfortable without encouraging the drowsiness that may result from lounging in an easy chair. Beware of squeaky rockers and chairs on casters. Try to situate yourself at a 90-degree angle from the narrator, so that you can look him/her in the eye and also glance occasionally at the recorder which is nearby. It should not be hidden, but neither should it be so conspicuous as to distract the narrator. Cushion the tape recorder and microphone with a sofa pillow, sweater, or some other soft material to reduce vibrations. Most microphones on modern equipment easily pick up voices from several feet away, and you want to avoid the intimidating gesture of thrusting the microphone under the subject's nose. You may need to use an extension cord to reach an appropriate electrical outlet.

Test the equipment before beginning, and also introduce each interviewing session with a simple statement such as, "This is an oral history interview with Mrs. Mary Brown in her home on July 14, 1975. The interviewer is Virginia Phelps." You may even want to precede the interview with a brief recording of small talk (this can be erased later) which can be played back to put the narrator at ease.

The Interview

Interviewing requires strenuous concentration, and one must exercise brain, eyes, ears, mouth, and even hands in various important and often simultaneous tasks. Maintain as much eye contact with the narrator as possible; this is an effective method of encouragement and reassurance. Your gently nodding head signals that you follow and appreciate what the narrator is saying. At the same time, periodically check the equipment to make sure that it is functioning properly and that the tape supply has not been exhausted. Follow the words carefully, listening for clues and references that suggest new lines of inquiry. Your brain and its memory will be taxed to store passing references and sudden ideas to retrieve at a later, more appropriate time. Your hands must operate the equipment and also make notes of the proper names mentioned by the narrator. The INTERVIEWER'S NOTES AND WORD LIST shown in figure 7 is vitally important to assure accuracy and to simplify the transcriptionist's job. A preferred method is to scribble a list of every proper name mentioned, spelling words phonetically when in doubt. Also write any special instructions to the transcriptionist. When the taping session is over ask the narrator to correct misspellings and supply full names. (Be careful here, however; one cannot rely absolutely on a narrator for correct spellings and full names.)

Who What Where When How and Why?

The interviewer's paramount objective is to help the narrator reconstruct his/her personal history with as much accuracy and vivid detail as possible. Every skill and prop employed to achieve this goal will significantly enhance the interview. Psychologists and gerontologists have discovered that a person's long-term memory does not fade with advancing age or even senility the way short-term memory does. Thus the chances are that the subject remembers a great deal about his/her life; the trick is to help retrieve it. Here are some tips for accomplishing that:

1. The right question. Ask provocative questions—who? what? where? when? how? why?

2. Employ cues. Ask about specific events or experiences. "What were you do- ing when the attack on Pearl Harbor was announced over the radio?" "Why did you vote for Roosevelt in 1936?"

3. Use props. Refer to family scrapbooks, photographs, newspaper clippings, heirlooms, artifacts, and maps. Be sure to identify and at least briefly de- scribe these on tape: "Here's a program from the 1939 New York World's Fair. How did you get it?" "This is a picture that I'd like to copy. Who is in it, and what was the occasion?"

4. Elicit emotions. Ask the narrator to recall his/her feelings about important personal experiences. "How did you feel about taking on a dangerous new job like that?"

5. The past as dialogue. Encourage the narrator to reconstruct conversations that were part of past experiences. People who are able to remember the past in terms of dialogue tend to exhibit vivid memories: "Then what did you say to your boss?"

6. Physical descriptions. At the beginning of any new topic ask the narrator to reconstruct in his/her mind's eye the physical appearance of familiar things ("Take me on an imaginary walking tour of the town square when you were a child"). Also, whenever a narrator indicates the size of some- thing vaguely or nonverbally such as gesturing with hands, ask for verbal clarification.

A: It fit into a container about like this.
Q: Is that roughly two feet long and six inches deep?
A: That's right, about the size of a dress box.

Be Patient

An occupational hazard among interviewers is impatience. Many persons feel uncomfortable after several seconds of silence and therefore jump in with a new question, often on a new topic. This is a mistake. Remember that the narrator may be stretching a memory back fifty years; he/she cannot be ex- pected to recapture and narrate such distant experiences fluently. Give the subject a chance to reflect and probe. If patience does not come naturally in such circumstances, time yourself to pause ten seconds before breaking the silence with a new question. You may be surprised to learn how often the narrator will recall some related incident if given the time to think about it.

Other Tips

Be careful not to exhaust the narrator. Few older persons are able to remi- nisce in this manner for more than an hour or maybe two.

Steadfastly avoid any questions that permit a simple yes or no reply. Instead of asking, "Did you fight in World War II?" you might ask, "What did you do during World War II?"

Questions should be simple, brief, and singular. Too often a novice asks questions that have at least several components. Refrain from rephrasing a question unless, after a lengthy silence or some other sign, it is evident that the narrator does not understand.

Do not interrupt if the response strays from the question. Let the narrator wander wherever his/her memory leads; you can always return later to a line of questioning.

Try at all costs to avoid interrupting the interview by turning the recorder off and on. Every time you operate the equipment during a taping session you run the risk of error and also remind the narrator of the taping; this can aggravate any nervousness or self-consciousness. If for some reason you must stop, include in the next recorded question some indication that taping stopped and is beginning again.

"While we had the recorder turned off for a few minutes you said you knew Carl Smith when he first came to town. Could you tell me about that?"

Use the interview outline as a general guide for questioning, but be flexible and alert enough to pursue new leads that may be dropped by the narrator. While some form of chronological order is desirable, no narrator can be expected to reconstruct the complexities and overlaps of a long period of time in correct historical sequence. With a good memory and some scribbled notes one can always return to an overlooked or bypassed topic.

After the Interview

Review the INTERVIEW NOTES AND WORD LIST with the narrator, comment encouragingly on the value of what has been gathered, make an appointment for the next taping session, and preview new topics.

It is prudent to label the tapes immediately, to help in record-keeping and to lessen the risk of loss. Write the narrator's name, date, and the number of each tape. This also is a good time to detach the two small plastic safety tabs in the back of the cassette, safeguarding against accidental erasure.

When the final taping session is finished, inform the narrator about subsequent steps, and their approximate length of time. Remind him/her of the opportunity to review the transcript after it has been edited (see Step 6: Finishing Touches, on page 63). Also mention whether the narrator will receive a complimentary copy of the tape or transcript, plus any other appropriate information.

The final task is to complete some important paperwork. Check spellings and names on the word list and make sure that the INTERVIEW DATA SHEET is filled out. Prepare three other forms:

The INTERVIEW CONTENTS SHEETS (figure 8) each represent a table of contents for the taped interviews, indicating the general subjects covered and the length of tape time in minutes. Select broad memoir topics (for example, "childhood years," "service during World War I"). Oral history interviews ramble too much to enable preparation of a comprehensive contents, but at least a general guide for listeners can be provided.

Any COLLATERAL MATERIALS received or reproduced should be listed and some items (notably photographs) should also be labeled. The inventory should include basic descriptive information as shown in the sample in figure 9.

Draft a summary statement known as INTERVIEWER'S COMMENTS (figure 10). This includes descriptions of the interview setting and the narrator, plus a candid evaluation of the narrator's veracity and the memoir's value.

With the interviewing and associated steps completed, one has finished the oral historian's job of *collection*. The product of these labors is a unique addition to our historical storehouse; one person's perishable memory has been converted to a permanent (tape) record. This is a significant and rewarding accomplishment, but it is only the beginning of the oral historian's job.

INTERVIEW CONTENTS

NARRATOR'S NAME McMann, Eldridge

TAPE NO 1

TIME			SUBJECTS
0	to	6	1. personal employment history
6		21	2. patients working in laundry
21	to	25	3. changes in laundry operations
25		30	4. laundry production
30	to	33	5. hiring practices
33		36	6. working schedule
36	to	40	7. Depression's effect on Jacksonville State Hospital
40		44	8. fire of 1929
44	to	46	9. new laundry building

Fig. 8. Sample Interview Contents sheet. (See also following page.)

Tri-County Historical Society

NARRATOR'S NAME Harold Johnson

TAPE NO. _1_

TIME		SUBJECTS
0 to 12	1.	Ancestors; birth and early years in
	2.	Brockington, Tennessee; schooling
12 to 16	3.	Summers working on uncle's farm;
	4.	farming practices
16 to 25	5.	World War I; war bond rallies;
	6.	treatment of German-Americans
25 to 31	7.	Move to Indianapolis; Indiana University;
	8.	college life in the 1920's
31 to 43	9.	First job--Fletcher Bank & Trust Co.;
	10.	loan and trust departments; banking practices
___ to ___	11.	in 1920's; Great Crash of 1929; loan defaults
	12.	& mortgage foreclosures; the 1933 bank
___ to ___	13.	holiday & New Deal laws
	14.	
43 to 45	15.	Family life during Depression
	16.	
SIDE Two 1 to 7	17.	Family life during Depression, cont.
	18.	
7 to 18	19.	Marriage in 1929; children;
	20.	decision to buy a home; buying
18 to 25	21.	Indianapolis during Depression;
	22.	WPA and work projects
25 to 31	23.	Bombing of Pearl Harbor; personal reaction;

Fig. 8 (cont.). Another sample Interview Contents sheet.

Tri-County Historical Society

COLLATERAL MATERIALS FOR: *Harold S. Johnson*

(Narrator's Name)

Instructions to the Interviewer:
Collateral materials, whether originals or copies, enhance the value
of an oral history memoir. Ask the narrator if you may borrow or keep
such things as personal photographs, newspaper clippings, pages from a
diary, and other mementos. Borrowed materials can be photographed or
duplicated and then returned.
List and describe all acquisitions below. A typical description
might be, "Copy of letter from Governor Henry Horner to James L. Singleton,
February 29, 1937." Provide as much identifying information for each
photograph as possible. Each photograph should be labeled on its back as
well as listed below.

1. *Photocopy of Johnson Family Bible -- Family tree*

2. *Photograph (circa 1922) of Harold S. Johnson and parents (Emmet and Gertrude Johnson), Brockington, Tennessee.*

3. *Photocopy of newspaper clipping, dated 10/11/34, Indianapolis Star.*

4. *Photocopy of letter of citation, dated 8/23/45, from Major*

5. *Robert Brown, U.S. Army Signal Corps.*

6.

7.

8.

9.

10.

11.

12.

13.

Fig. 9. A Collateral Materials list.

Tri-County Historical Society
_____

INTERVIEWER'S COMMENTS

Harold Johnson
_____ Memoir
(Narrator's Name)

Interviewer's observations about the interview setting, physical description
   of the narrator, comments on narrator's veracity and accuracy, and
   candid assessment of the historical value of the memoir.

NOTE: Use parentheses ( ) to enclose any words, phrases or sentences that
   should be regarded as confidential.

        The interviews took place in the living room of Mr. Johnson's home
on 38th Street in Indianapolis. It is a quiet neighborhood, and the home
is comfortably furnished with family furniture. Mr. Johnson sat in his
favorite reading chair.

        Harold Johnson is 67 years old; he has been retired from the banking
business for six years. He appears to be in good health for his age, though
he did tire quickly after about an hour of conversation. He talks a lot
about his family and he has many pictures of children, grandchildren, etc.

        (His memory is irregular. Some things are vivid in his mind, others
are unclear or totally forgotten. Photographs and other props help
somewhat, but he has trouble remembering the details of personal experiences.)

        (Generally his recollections seem credible to me. He had no discernible
axe to grind, except for some bitter comments about his employer at the time
of his involuntary retirement.) He is at his best talking about everyday
social life, including schooling, holidays, family occasions and the cultural
life of his community.

        9/10/75   Jane Rogers
      _____   _____
      (Date)   (Interviewer's Name)

Fig. 10. The Interviewer's Comments.

Exercise 2: Interviewing Technique

A. Following are brief passages from three interviews conducted for the John F. Kennedy Library.* In each case the questioner demonstrates one or more failings in interview technique. Identify and diagnose these mistakes.

(1)

Q. The President also appointed you to serve on his own Committee for Equal Employment Opportunity, a matter about which the President felt strongly. How did the President approach this problem?

A: He took it very seriously. He understood how deeply important the question of jobs and fairness in hiring, and fairness in promotion in jobs—how desperately important this is for its bearing on all kinds of other problems in this nation. As you know, one of the first actions that President Kennedy took upon his assumption of office was the combination of two committees which had previously existed: a committee on government employment within the federal service and a second committee, which had been, under previous administration, concerned with employment in that sector of industry which is under contract with the federal government. These two committees were combined into a new committee, strengthened by the appointments he made of a number of outstanding individuals. Vice President Johnson was made the chairman, and an Executive Order was issued which really put the power into the hands of this committee to do the job. It had the power to abrogate any contract which failed to observe stringent provisions of fairness in equal employment. When the committee was formed thus with this power, the President began its work by himself appearing in the Cabinet room of the White House to talk to us about what this meant to our national life, what it meant to him, and what he would require of every member of that committee, the Cabinet members and all the others. No substitutes, he said, would be allowed. He wanted us to come personally and to work at the job—no nonsense about it. We were all moved; we were all deeply impressed; and under Vice President Johnson the committee went to work to do the best job that it knew how.

Q: Finally, how do you evaluate him as a man—his impact on the international scene, on this country, on the youth of this country and elsewhere, et cetera?

(2)

Q: How did she impress you as a person when you first saw her?

A: My impression of Mrs. Kennedy first was, to be perfectly frank, that here is a young woman who has a lot to learn about an institution like this. But she learned it rapidly and gracefully.

Q: And she was very interested in learning, wasn't she?

*Memoir excerpts courtesy of the John F. Kennedy Library, Cambridge, Mass.

A: Very interested in doing it, indeed.

Q: And easy to work with?

A: Oh, yes, easy to work with, and not only easy to work with, but happy to work with you.

(3)

Q: How often did you run into the President? Do you happen to remember that?

A: Not too often, the President. I'd pass him sometimes in the hallway, but I had much more to do with Mrs. Kennedy.

Q: You worked for her on the Fine Arts Committee, is that right?

A: Yes, I did.

Q: Doing the upholstery?

A: That's right.

Q: Well, what were her tastes like? Did she seem to know exactly what she wanted?

A: Marvelous taste, marvelous. She seemed to know a little bit about everything whether it was materials or paintings. I never saw anyone like that for her age. She was wonderful.

Q: And you thought she was an intelligent woman?

A: Oh, yes.

B. In the following excerpts from an oral history memoir what methods does the interviewer employ to help the narrator reconstruct his personal history in graphic detail?

Q: Would you tell me when you were born and your parents' names?

A: My parents' names—my father's name was Peter Campo. My mother's name was Antoinette LaRocca.

Q: Were they both born here in Springfield?

A: No, in Italy. I was born in Italy myself. Born and raised in Italy.

Q: Which province?

A: I was—I'm from Sicily.

Q: Then you were born in what year? Or what was your birth date?

A: 1894—December 25, 1894. I always said Jesus and I were born at the same time. (laughter)

Q: When did you come to this country? Or why did your father decide to come to this country?

A: My father didn't come to this country.

Q: Your father did not?

A: No. I came to this country. I had two brothers here, and things were a little rough in Sicily. I decided I wanted to come over here. And I did come here; I came here in 1912. I left there on May the 10th, 1912. It was the day after Easter—of April, April the 10th, I left Italy. On the ninth was Easter and the morning after Easter I left and I came to this country.

Q: Where were your brothers living at that time?

A: One was living in Springfield and one in Farmersville right south of here.

Q: Why did they happen to come to this area?

A: Well, I had a cousin of mine here that was here, and so he was writing back and forth, and naturally, I came here so they had somebody they knew.

Q: Were they working in the mines?

A: In the coal mines, yes. I worked in the coal mines, and I worked on the railroads. I worked on this line here that's just a half a block from here. That was the C. & A. then; now it's the G. M. & O. It was Chicago and Alton, that's what the C. & A. is, the Chicago and Alton.

Q: You were eighteen years old?

A: I was about seventeen and a half years old. My birthday is on Christmas, and I came here in April.

Q: Were you scared when you left home?

A: No. No, I was not. But I had a very bad trip—I had a very bad experience on my trip. For one thing, I caught bad cold, and my eyes were watering so bad, they were sticking and everything else. And I was seasick all the way through from Naples—in fact, from Palermo, we take the night, the mail boat, to Naples and then from Naples we take the boat to this country. It took us fourteen days to travel here.

Q: And you took the boat from Sicily first.

A: From Palermo, which is Sicily, to Naples. That's mail boat. Then you take the regular passenger ship to come here. And as I say, I got—I was seasick all the time—fortunate that I had a couple of older people that would bring me a little food to the bed and everything else. Then I got this infection in my eyes— I couldn't hardly see, I had to wash my eyes every few minutes—and there was, in those days, if you didn't have perfect eyesight—no infection in your eyes at all—you couldn't leave Italy. They examined you before you leave— you have to have perfect eyes, otherwise, they wouldn't let you come on.

Q: Why?

A: Well, because I guess they had a ruling in this country—they didn't want no eye infections or something like that. So . . .

Q: It was this country, you think, that . . .

A: I suppose it was this country, yes. So what happens—land in New York and they took us to what they call—island.

Q: Ellis?

A: Ellis Island—and we were in a big room—about, oh, must have been 750 to 800 people, all of us, sitting there waiting—and they gave us a little box, it cost us $1.00, they had a couple of bananas and four or five sandwiches and this and that to take you for the trip. So pretty soon, somebody calls my name, and they took me in a room, there was three of us, three people. And they call some woman that had left her husband without her husband's consent. And they says, "You've got to go back." So, you know, I hear that, and me with my eyes. Pretty soon, they called this man and they said that the law wanted him over in Sicily—he had to go back. And I thought to myself, "Well, I'm going back." And I figured, "If I'm going to have to do that—those bad trips I had—I'll jump overboard and drown myself." That's how discouraged I was. Nevertheless, they asked me a lot of questions and everything else, where I was going, who I was coming to see and this and that and the other, and then they said, "Okay. It's all right, that's fine." I got on the train, they give you a plaque, just about, oh, about this wide and just about this long.

Q: About two by four inches?

A: Yes. They put here for your destination, where you're going, your name; your destination and this and that and the other. Well, I got on the train in New York and we changed trains—I don't know where, but when we went to change trains, I think it might have been to St. Louis, I'm not sure because we come in on the Chicago and Alton from the south, so it had to be St. Louis probably—I went for my grip, and my grip's gone. So all the clothes I got— just what I got on. That's all I had. (laughter)

Q: Did you ever find your grip?

A: No. I didn't even know how to look for it or anything. It wasn't there and that was it. Somebody grabbed it.

Q: Can you describe the conditions on shipboard for me? How did you live on that ship?

A: Well, those days were bad. They were bad, and now conditions are different. I've went back since then, but they were bad. The food wasn't very good and they weren't too clean, and the water wasn't fresh water. Now you use fresh water because it's sterilized water. They had a lot of water when they started. It was just sea water, and it was greasy. You wash your utensils, your dishes and everything else—it was just greasy—just bad. Bad, very bad.

Q: How many of you slept in one room?

A: Well, we had bunks. I think there was four in each place. Below and up, below and up because they're narrow places.

Q: You were pretty crowded.

A: Yes, very much.

Q: What class did you travel? Do you remember?

A: (laughter) Last class. (laughter)

Q: Last class? What they call steerage?

A: I suppose, I suppose. In those days it cost to come over here—I think it cost me $18.00 for the trip.

Q: $18.00!

A: Yes.

Q: Did you have money in your pocket?

A: Well, I came here into Springfield with $6.00 in my pocket.

Q: How much did you start out with from Sicily?

A: Oh, probably $10.00.

Q: Had that been a struggle to collect that $10.00?

A: Maybe $10.00–$12.00. No, my father gave it to me when I left there. My father, God bless his soul, he treated me in some way a little better than the rest of the kids, because if I tell you my story now, you'll see why. But he always was good to me, and he hated me (to go)—I had an argument with him for two months before he consented me for my passport. Finally, he let me go.

Q: It must have been hard on both your father and mother to send the third son over.

A: My mother was already dead.

Q: How many children were there in your family?

A: Eleven—nine brothers and two sisters.

Q: How many eventually came over to this country?

A: Well, I think it was—let's see, three, four, five, six—seven.

Q: The rest stayed in Sicily?

A: Yes. Two of them stayed in Sicily and one is dead now—died last year—and one is in South America—in Venezuela—which I went to visit him last August.

Q: After you got off the train at Springfield—did you come all the way to Springfield?

A: Got off the train at Springfield and . . .

Q: Who met you?

A: Nobody. Unfortunately. There was a policeman there—there was a policeman there, and I was showing him (my name tag), and he says, "Come on with me." And took me just about a half block east on Washington Street—there used to be a fruit store there, fellow by the name of Rochalli, he was an Italian guy—so he took me in there and this guy called a cousin of mine that lived on Carpenter Street and they come and picked me up.

Q: What did your tag say exactly? The name . . .

A: My name and my destination.

Q: It said Springfield?

A: Yes, yes.

Q: And then what—you started out living with this cousin?

A: No. I went and got myself a room, boarding with some people. I had one little room not quite as big as this, and I had a little stove there.

Q: About ten feet by ten feet, maybe?

A: That's about it. And I had a little old bunk there, and a little small table. The stove was one that they call a "Peter," like a pear, with a bulge in the middle, you know, a coal stove with a pipe that sticks out and everything else.

Q: You called it a "Peter" stove?

A: Yes. I remember I used to—well, now I'm going too far on that—I should tell you what I did after that. All right, I was here about three days and I went to see a friend of mine that lived around Third and Carpenter along the track there, and I told him that I'd like to get a job of some kind, any kind, with me, I'd take any kind of a job. All my life I've said I'd take any kind of a job, just so I work. So he said to me, "Well," he said, "I'll tell you. We've got a car of cabbages over here on the track, just about a half block from here." He says, "We got to unload it. If you help me, why, it'll be all right. You'll get paid for it." We went in there and there isn't any more—anything—that stinks worse than rotten cabbages. Well, you see, they can't—I don't know how far they been traveling—some get bad

EXERCISE 3: REHEARSING WITH A PRACTICE MEMOIR

A. Before embarking on your first formal interview, try the preliminaries and interviewing with a practice memoir. Select someone (a friend, relative, or neighbor) who is willing to help with this rehearsal. Go through all the preliminary steps (see Step 1: Getting Ready), then conduct a short (maximum fifteen minutes) interview on some specific event or experience in the subject's life. It may help to pick a dramatic experience, like the Pearl Harbor or Kennedy assassination announcements. Follow the instructions and advice in Step 2: Interviewing.

B. Arrange for an experienced oral historian or another student to evaluate your practice memoir as follows:

Evaluator's Report: . . . . by . . . .
                (Interviewer)   (Evaluator)

The taped interview:

1. Is the recording clear and free of extraneous noises?
2. Are the questions simple, clear, and direct?
3. Cite instances of good and bad interviewing technique.
4. Did the questions elicit specific and vivid responses?

Checklist of forms and procedures:

1. Legal release OK?
2. Interview data sheet OK?
3. Contact notes OK?
4. Interview outline OK?
5. Interviewer's notes and word list OK?
6. Interviewer's comments OK?
7. Any collateral materials? Comment.

Additional remarks:

III

Processing
Oral
History

The oral history interview produces historical material in taped form, but as long as it remains available in only that form it may be little used. The typewritten transcript is a more conveniently used form and provides for wider usage.

How Much Processing?

The lengths to which a program goes in processing oral history interviews depend on time and budget limitations. Some programs begin and end with the typing of a rough transcript; others perform several further steps in order to produce a more polished document. The rough transcript is audited, edited, and perhaps rearranged into chronological or topical order. Following a careful reading to ensure its semantic flow, the transcript is taken to the narrator for correction and approval. After return to the oral history office, the transcript is read again to make sure that readability has not been diminished and that the narrator's changes will be clear to the final typist. A preface and title page are prepared and along with the transcript are typed in final form. When the final copy is proofread and necessary corrections are made, a table of contents and index are prepared and typed. Then the memoir is copied or printed and bound in some fashion. The final copy may be sent to the narrator for his/her signature before or after it is duplicated. A finished transcript may include extras such as collateral materials and the narrator's photograph as a frontispiece.

What Kind of Processing?

Regardless of the lengths to which one goes in processing, it is necessary to decide what kind of processing to do, what kind of transcripts to prepare. To some extent the kind of transcript prepared is determined by the program's purpose and the image one wishes to project of the program and narrators. At one extreme are programs whose professional historian-interviewers seek out only well-known persons or authoritative eyewitnesses to specific historical eras or events. Transcriptionists type verbatim transcripts; editors polish grammar and syntax to conform to academically expected patterns and, to some extent, to protect narrators' egos. The final textbooklike transcripts present the facts and read smoothly, but possibly lifelessly.

At the other extreme are programs which interview almost anyone willing to talk and amass a collection of memoirs that make enjoyable reading but may contain little of historical value. Such an approach to interviewing may be accompanied by a desire to present people "just as they are." Transcriptionists, typing literally verbatim transcripts, try to recreate the speakers' dialects or accents and to reflect the sound and pace of the interview. Editors, being uncritical of the narrators' rhetoric, limit their work to a check on spelling and punctuation. The final transcripts of such programs present the facts; but, far from conforming to academically or even commonly accepted patterns, they may be difficult to read.

What Do Users Want?

The decision of what kind of transcripts to prepare should be based in part on the needs of users; those needs differ but are not contradictory. Some will read an oral history transcript only for the historical information it contains. They will want a transcript that is verbatim and that is presented in an easy-to-read fashion. Other users will want a transcript which reveals, in addition to the facts, the speakers' individualities and the tone of the interview, whether formal or informal. The means to preparing a transcript that will satisfy both kinds of users and will suit the purposes of most programs lie somewhere between the two extremes previously described.

The Ideal Transcript

The ideal transcript is an accurate verbatim reflection of the interview's content, preserves as much of the quality of the interview and the individualities of the speakers as possible, and is easy to read and understand.

In order to achieve this kind of transcript, the program's staff must have more than typing skills and knowledge of the rules of grammar and punctuation that apply to written language. They must also appreciate the raw material they are working with—spoken language. They must learn to retain the essential and desirable qualities of spoken language and refine or delete less essential ones while shaping the interview into a different form, the written transcript. The following instructions for the various processing steps were written to help each worker understand what his/her task entails, and how, in doing that task, the differences between spoken and written language can be reconciled within a transcript.

Recording the Process

The INTERVIEW DATA SHEET on which the interviewer has recorded biographical and interview information serves as a work sheet which tells at a glance the processing status of each interview from the time the tape is brought to the office. Reference is made to the INTERVIEW DATA SHEET in each of the following processing sections to show how each step is recorded. Figure 11 shows the dates on which tapes were received and labeled and that the collateral materials were filed.

Step 3: Transcribing

Getting the Facts

The oral history transcriptionist's main task is to type an accurate verbatim transcript of the interview. This means typing the interview contents—all the words and transcribable sounds on the tape—just as they occur on the tape. It is essential to type words in their order of occurrence. Be careful; misordered words can drastically change the meaning of some sentences and distort the facts the speaker intended to convey. Consider the following example:

> He also was responsible for that error.
> He was also responsible for that error.
> He was responsible for that error also.

Conveying Speech

A second part of the transcriptionist's job is to type a transcript which reflects the conversational quality of spoken language and each speaker's individuality.

When people speak in conversation, they usually express themselves more spontaneously than when they write. They are less careful about grammar and sentence construction, and less precise about pronunciation and enunciation than they would be about spelling if they were writing. Therefore, a verbatim transcript of spoken words would be more casual and less precise than the written expression of the same ideas.

The physical voice can portray a speaker's age, social and regional background, intelligence, and sensitivity. In any transcribing process some of those elements of individuality are lost when the voice disappears. To some extent, however, the transcriptionist can retain those elements and convey them to the reader. This is done by accurately reflecting a speaker's choice of words and the arrangement of those words within sentences. Forget about using correct

Tri-County Historical Society
INTERVIEW DATA SHEET

This section is to be completed by the Interviewer.

NARRATOR _Harold S. Johnson_ ADDRESS _1127 38th Street, Indianapolis, Indiana_ PHONE _643-8812_

BIRTHDATE _4/12/08_ BIRTHPLACE _Brockington, Tennessee_ INTERVIEWER _Jane Rogers_ PHONE _342-4461_

DATE(S) & PLACE OF INTERVIEW(S) _7/14/75 7/20 7/24 8/3 Narrator's home_

COLLATERAL MATERIAL Yes ☑ No ☐   TERMS _Open_

- -

This section is for office use. Write the date in the larger columns and check the smaller ones to record each process.

TAPES	Received & Labeled	Collaterals Filed	Transcribing — Begun	Transcribing — No. of Pages	Transcribing — Total Time	Catalogued	Audited	Editing — Begun	Editing — Total Time	Review — To Narrator	Returned	Reread	Preface	Final Typing — Begun	Text Finished	Index, Table of Contents	Proofread	Corrected	Duplicating Transcript — Sent	Returned	Duplicating Tape — Sent	Returned	Shelf Copy	Narrator's Copy	NUCMC	Microfilm	Radio
1	7-22-75 ✓	✓	10/20/75	37	8½hr	✓	✓	12-3-75	0¾hr	1-7-76	✓ 1-7-76	✓	✓	✓ 2-21-76	✓	✓	✓	✓	✓ 3-11-76	✓	✓ 12-14-76	✓					
2	7-22-75 ✓	✓	10/22/75	34	8 hr	✓	✓	12-5-75	0		✓	✓					✓		"		"						
3	8-9-75 ✓	✓	10/24/75	38	8½hr	✓	✓	12-6-75	10hr		✓	✓					✓		"		"						
4	"	✓	10/25/75	14	3¾hr	✓	✓	12-10-75	4½hr		✓	✓	✓	✓	✓	✓	✓	✓	"	✓	"	✓					
5	"	✓	10/26/75	36	8¼hr	✓	✓	12-10-75	19										"		"						

Fig. 11. The lower half of the Interview Data Sheet indicating interview's processing status.

word forms and proper sentence construction if the speakers did. Type "we was" or "it taken longer than we thought," if that's what was said. Type contractions and abbreviations when they were used. Run several sentences together if the speaker did.

Ordinarily, a transcriptionist refrains from cleaning up the elements of speech—that is the editor's job. However, programs which use a rough transcript as the final users' copy might grant transcriptionists editorial license to delete, insert, or rearrange words in order to improve the transcript's clarity and readability. For the program which can go further with processing, it is best to begin with a verbatim rough transcript which reflects all the words and sounds as they are on the tape.

Spelling words correctly and completely is not a form of cleaning up, however; that is part of the transcriptionist's task. Some would argue that typing a verbatim transcript requires that one misspell words to reflect regional differences in pronunciation and drop word endings to reflect the casual nature of spoken language. For some purposes reflecting dialect in this way is essential for accurately portraying a speaker. Some of the current books based on oral history interviews portray dialect and do it effectively. But since the oral history transcript can usually be augmented by listening to the tape if the reader wants to know more about dialect, thinking of how to type improper spellings and inventing contractions is only time-consuming. More importantly, such unfamiliar "words" can impede reading.

Mispronounced significant words sometimes require exception to the rule of correct spelling, especially when they are consistently mispronounced. If you deliberately misspell a word, you *must* make a marginal note of this and state your reason. An example is the colloquial pronunciation, Meredosh, for Meredosia, Illinois. The editor will decide whether to change the spelling or to incorporate your note in a footnote. As long as you make note of your action, that decision can be made and the "error" you made deliberately and for good reason will not later confuse or mislead readers. Resist the temptation to misspell in order to simply reflect the quaintness of a speaker.

The words "yeah" and "yes" may require cleaning up. In general, a transcriptionist should type yes to indicate an affirmative reply because, on the printed page, yeah easily implies cynicism and toughness. Yes may seem stilted and be a slightly inaccurate reflection of an interview's casual nature, but it is more likely to be correctly interpreted. However, when transcribing a related conversation, it is acceptable to transcribe yeah if it is a suitable reflection of cynicism, toughness, surprise, or some other emotion. In the following examples, yeah is used appropriately.

> We told the director we'd be ready for opening night but he said, "Yeah? I'll believe it when the curtain goes up."

> I was the spokesman for the guys on our shift and when I tells the boss there was sure to be trouble if we didn't get no pay raise he says, "Oh, yeah? We'll see who has trouble."

They said they'd be out to see me in an hour. I was shocked. I said, "Yeah? Wow! Okay."

False Starts

Because people are less concise as speakers than as writers, they often make false starts and repeat a word or phrase before they get their point across. Transcribe false starts and repetitions; omitting such elements of spoken language is an error, just as is cleaning up poor grammar. The editor may have to delete some false starts and repetitions to make the transcript easier to read, but those that are important either to meaning or to portrayal of the speaker should be retained.

Crutch Words

There are two varieties of crutch words, the *pauser* and the *elicitor*. Pausers are common in spoken language because people unconsciously or self-consciously use them to fill silences created when they pause to think. In the oral history interview these may occur even more frequently because speakers may feel more self-conscious than usual. Most pausers should be transcribed; the following will help to decide which ones.

One kind of pauser is *stammering*; it need not be transcribed. The first sentence below shows a literally verbatim transcription; the second sentence shows what should have been transcribed.

> I-I tri-took the man in and tried to help him but he was not coop-uncooperative so we didn-couldn't help.

> I took the man in and tried to help him but he was uncooperative so we couldn't help.

A second kind of pauser is *a gutteral sound*. Transcribe those that express surprise or sudden understanding. The following example shows a correct transcription.

Q: Ah, then when he met you, he met you in New York!

However, if "Ah" were used only to fill time and had no relationship to the sentence, it should not have been transcribed.

Transcribe gutteral sounds that help to indicate that the speaker, especially the narrator, was in a real emotional or intellectual quandary.

A: After that, oh, I guess after three or four years, I was employed in service.

Q: You were employed in service?

A: In, uh, what do you call it? Well, I guess you'd call that, uh, working with people in homes.

Q: Oh, you were employed as a domestic?

A: Domestic, yes. That's what I wanted to say.

Interviewers frequently utter supportive sounds like mmm, hmm, and uh-huh. Do not transcribe them.

A third kind of pauser is *the habitually used word*. Some examples are: and, but, well, so, anyway, don't you know, you know, and like. They may be introductory words at the beginnings of sentences or be interjected mid-sentence. Transcribe all of them. If they are used meaninglessly or too frequently, the editor will probably delete some to improve readability, but enough will be retained to show that they are part of a speaker's speech pattern.

Elicitors are the other variety of crutch word. It may just be the habit of a speaker to say words such as "you see." But the use of such words may be a meaningful request for an assurance of understanding; if so, they should be transcribed.

The interviewer may respond to the narrator's elicitors with a gutteral sound or by saying "yes." Such responses should not be transcribed unless a narrator actually stopped to wait for a response. In that case, transcribe the interviewer's gutteral sounds as yes or no, even though that may appear stilted.

Q: What part of a hog do you use to make sausage?

A: That was the offals of all the trimming. Now, like the shoulder, now, a hog has a shoulder and a side and a ham, you know. And when you quartered it up like that, you know, we'd take our knife and go around. . . . You know how nice a ham is, you've bought hams, you know?

Q: Yes.

A: Well, when they cut that off, there's a square. We'd take this fat off here, don't you see, and cut that up into lard.

Emotion and Action

When people speak they use more than words to communicate their messages; they use faces and hands, but those means of expression cannot be recorded. Expressions of emotions are means of communication, too, and are important to listeners, and to the reader of a transcript, because they qualify or emphasize words.

Audible expressions of emotion and action can be transcribed by typing a note to the reader about what is being heard. Use as few words as possible and place them in parentheses; no capitalization or periods are necessary. Some examples are:

> (laughs) when one speaker does
> (laughter) when both participants do
> (pounds fist on table)

(walks away from microphone; part of response is inaudible)
(tape turned off and on again)

If a speaker has the habit of laughing nervously, don't transcribe such laughter unless it shows evidence of a real dilemma.

Punctuation

Part of our spoken message is conveyed through emphatic pauses, inflection, and tone of voice. These can be communicated through punctuation so effectively that a reader can soon catch the rhythm of the speaker's voice and accurately emphasize important words.

It is extremely important to *punctuate a transcript for clarity of meaning.* Use the usual rules of punctuation when possible, and the minimum amount of punctuation required to achieve clarity. The rules of style, given in appendix B of this manual, and a grammar book will undoubtedly prove helpful.

It is also important to *convey sound or silence through punctuation.* However, caution must be taken to not cloud a sentence's meaning or damage readability. Commas are the form of punctuation most commonly used to convey pauses or to show that a phrase was emphasized. They tell a reader "pause here" or "watch out now, the following is a little different." But there are other forms of punctuation—the dash and the three points of the ellipsis—which can be used when using additional commas might confuse the reader. When used carefully together in a transcript, each punctuation mark can come to convey a different *length* of pause and a different *degree* of difference. The shortest pause and least degree of difference are implied by the comma. The dash (two hyphens typed together) means a slightly longer pause and a greater degree of difference. Use the three points of the ellipsis mid-sentence, and the period followed by the three points after a sentence, to convey a really long pause; but use these *sparingly* (see appendix B).

Inflection and tone of voice can be conveyed through the exclamation point, but be careful not to use it too frequently or it will lose its impact upon the reader. If underlining is used in this way, its use should also be kept to a minimum.

Typing Instructions

The preceding pages have explained how it is possible to produce a transcript that reflects the words of the interview and, as well, the conversational quality of spoken language and the individualities of speakers. What follows are instructions for typing transcripts. They show a range of possibilities on some points, so are more lengthy than the actual instructions needed by any transcriptionist. Tailor your program's instructions to reflect your own practices.

1. Check out a tape to transcribe and write the beginning date on the INTERVIEW DATA SHEET. Keep a cumulative record of the time spent and attach it to the transcript. Record this time on the INTERVIEW DATA SHEET when you

finish the transcript (see figure 11). This information is valuable in figuring costs in budgeting and other program management procedures.

2. Also check out the INTERVIEWER'S NOTES AND WORD LIST, INTERVIEWER'S COMMENTS, INTERVIEW CONTENTS sheet, and any other available material to help in the accurate transcription of difficult proper names, unfamiliar terms, and so on. Be careful not to misplace any of these items; they are primary historical documents which cannot be replaced.

3. Before beginning to transcribe, read the INTERVIEWER'S COMMENTS which usually contain directions for transcriptionists.

4. Listen to about fifteen minutes of the tape to become familiar with the subject matter and to get the feel of the interview—to understand the accents and to recognize the speech patterns and mannerisms. At this time begin to plan how you will use punctuation to reflect the interview as faithfully as possible.

5. As you transcribe, listen to a few words or a phrase and then type. Listen far enough ahead to avoid "putting words in the speakers' mouths." Anticipating the speakers' words might result in an error of factual significance or cause a change in wording or sentence structure. Listening ahead will also help you to punctuate correctly, that is, to avoid ending a sentence when the narrator merely paused mid-sentence or stopped for breath. By listening ahead you will be able to identify topical changes which require new paragraphs.

6. A neat and accurate transcript is more important than a speedy job. Because transcribing is the first step in processing, it is the basis for all the work that will follow. A good rough transcript will ease and speed each succeeding step. In addition, it will be less frustrating to both the narrator and final typist if they receive an accurately typed transcript which has required a minimum of editor's marks.

7. When you make errors, correct them. Do not make strikeovers. The chalky-paper correction products are good to use on one or two mistyped letters. Make more extensive corrections by crossing out the entire wrong word with the upper case X. Some programs use a chalky-liquid correction product to correct extensive errors.

8. Be accurate about spelling; use reference books, your office's list of problematical words, and the INTERVIEWER'S NOTES AND WORD LIST. Some helpful aids are a good dictionary, *Who's Who,* or a book on the subject matter, especially for technical terms.

9. Expect to have difficulty transcribing some interviews. Background noise or electrical interference may have made part of a tape inaudible. When an interview involves more than two people, keeping names and voices straight can be a problem. A speaker's voice level may rise and fall to such an extent that it is difficult to find a comfortable constant volume at which to transcribe. Some speakers habitually mumble inaudibly at the ends of sentences. Dialects and accents may be hard to understand; colloquial speech and professional jargon may be so unfamiliar that you cannot make sense of what was said.

There are ways to overcome such difficulties. For clues, refer to the INTER-VIEWER'S NOTES AND WORD LIST. Replay a troublesome section several times at various speeds and volumes. If the transcriber has a speaker, listen to that section aloud. If you have earphones as well as the machine's headset, try those. Use another transcribing machine if one is available. Ask co-workers for help; it is not uncommon in an oral history office to see several staff members huddled around a transcribing machine, straining to understand a difficult section. If you still can't figure it out, type a line the approximate length of the missing portion and the auditor, editor, or narrator may be able to fill it in later. If you have any idea what it might be, pencil in your thoughts. Sometimes the meaning becomes clear later; in that case, go back and fill in the blanks.

Typing Specifications

1. Make an original and one carbon copy of each page. The carbon is a safety measure in case the original is lost during the succeeding steps of processing. Some programs make only one copy, the original. After editing it, they make a photocopy of it to send to the narrator and retain the original. Other programs make an original and one carbon, filing the carbon as is to serve as historical documentation of the original transcription; the original copy is edited and then duplicated. The duplicate is retained as documentation of changes made by the editor. The edited original is sent to the narrator for review and it is retained, after the final copy is typed from it, as documentation of changes made by the narrator.

2. Triple space between lines to allow adequate space for auditor's and editor's work and narrator's changes.

3. Indent the first line of a new paragraph five spaces.

4. Margins: left, 1½ inch; right, 1 inch; top and bottom, 1 inch. Some programs double space and leave wider margins in which to make editorial marks. Triple spacing and making marks and corrections in and above the lines of type seem to result in a transcript which is more easily deciphered by narrators, few of whom have had editorial experience.

5. Type the following identifying information at the left margin on the first page:

Narrator's name:
Tape number:
Date of interview:
Place of interview:
Interviewer's name:
For: (name of institution)

If this information is not on the tape, get it from the INTERVIEW DATA SHEET. Triple space down and type the first line of the interview.

6. Type the following identifying information on the first line of the second and each succeeding page: narrator's name; tape number (at the left margin);

page number (at the right margin). Each person's memoir, whether a single interview on one tape or a series of interviews on several tapes, should be consecutively paginated.

7. Use a question/answer format, identifying interviewer's questions and comments as Q: and narrator's responses as A:. Type a colon after the letter, double space after the colon. The second line of a Q: or an A: should be typed even with the left margin. For interviews that involve more than two narrators or two interviewers, use Q: or A: and the initials of each narrator or interviewer, Q:/A.C./E.C.; A:/E.C./A.C. If a friend or family member occasionally enters into the interview, identify that person by name, Q:/A:/ Mrs. Toigo. Alternatives to the question/answer format are:

Interviewer:/Interviewee:
Last name of interviewer:/Last name of narrator:
Initials of interviewer/Initials of narrator:

8. Upon reaching the end of the first side of a tape, indicate that by typing END OF SIDE ONE three lines down, at the left margin and in capital letters. Space down three lines before typing SIDE TWO at the left margin. Upon completing the tape, space down three lines and type END OF TAPE at the left margin. Space down three lines and type your name, Transcriptionist.

When you finish typing the transcript, file it, the tape, INTERVIEWER'S NOTES AND WORD LIST, and so on. Record the total number of transcript pages and the total transcribing time on the INTERVIEW DATA SHEET as shown in figure 11.

Figures 12 and 13 are sample rough transcript pages. Both contain errors which will be corrected in later steps of processing.

Step 4: Auditing

Auditing, the proofreading of the rough transcript against the tape, is done after transcribing and before editing. Even if the program goes no further in processing than preparing a rough transcript, an audit should be performed to be certain the transcript accurately reflects the interview. In addition, during this step obvious spelling and typographical errors can be caught and corrected.

Who Should Audit?

The question of whether auditing should be done by a person assigned to only that task or should be part of the transcriptionist's or editor's duties is one that should be considered. Because it is an exacting and tedious job, it should probably not be assigned to any one person as a full-time job. Some programs ask a person employed in a secretarial or clerical task to spend part of his/ her workday auditing.

If transcriptionists are asked to audit their own work, a program runs a

Larry Mantowich (3)   142

You can have one per cent, one-tnth of one per cent of carbon monox-

ide, and you still have a smoldering fire. You got to have a hundred

per cent CO^2 before you can break that seal and start operations

again.

Q: So when you seal a mine you sometimes seal it with this cloth?

A: No, that's a ...

Q: That's just a temporary measure to get to the fire?

A: Yes. A braddish XXXX cloth is . . . if you had a deep room some-

place and it wasn't getting enough air, you put a braddish cloth

across the entry. Instead of the air going straight in, it'll turn

and go into this deep room, see. Just to divert the air, change the

current, course of air. But I remember at Dall Coal Company where we

had a fire. XXXXXXXXX You know I told you we had to seal this live

mule in the mine. Well, you seal off the entire hole where the cage

is at. You just board it across and trowel wood fiber or whatever

it is over XX the top of this hole.

Well, you leave a pipe, a three inch pipe or any opening pipe, capped

off like any other pipe. They way we did it, we had magnesium

Fig. 12. A sample rough draft as it appears upon completion by the transcriptionist.

Larry Mantowich (3)   145

A: Yes. And another funny thing in the mine, if a guy got on a drunk

or something, and he was in . . . . Because when you went in the mine

if you was going to load . . . . I remember when at Barr Coal Company

the _____ was two guys working together. They had to load

forty cars. That's twenty ton apiece. Well, they started sweating

from the first thing in the morning and they'd sweat until noon, and

eat dinner and then they'd sweat until quitting time agian. They'd

sweat all day long. Then if they was on a drunk or something . . .

and you could walk in that room and tha'ts all you could smell. Pure

alcohol. (laughter) Another funny thing. If you was walking the

_____ a last open crosscutt, a little bit too far, why, they

call that working ahead of air. Well, you're working in a bottled up

place there, and you could, you'd have to leave your open light back

at the crosscut and get in there with you ___coat___ first thing

in the morning and fan yourface out so you'd mix up your air because

that would be a pocket of gas in there. So if you'd fan it with your

coat, well, then that would mix it up with air, and then you wouldn't

light this gas. And if you didn't have very much air in your room and

Fig. 13. Another rough sample transcript page.

greater risk of having mistyped words and similar errors go unnoticed and being compounded in succeeding steps. A transcriptionist must be critical of his/her own work and listen closely for differences rather than listening to ascertain correctness. Using a different transcriber, or a headset instead of earphones, might help the transcriptionist catch errors made because of poor sound quality. It is less tiring for a transcriptionist to audit a few pages at a time after they are typed than to do it all at the end.

When auditing is done by the editor or another person, there is the advantage that the tape will be heard by fresh ears. Even so, the auditor should be a critical listener and guard against being lulled into expecting to hear what was typed. An auditor-editor would become familiar with the speakers' speech patterns and mannerisms, which is a necessary preliminary to editing. In addition, the auditor-editor could use this time to catch the most obvious typographical errors and errors in punctuation and spelling. More complete editing would follow.

Auditing Instructions

One's task as auditor is to proofread the transcript against the tape. By simultaneously listening to the tape and reading the transcript, make certain that the transcript is an accurate and complete representation of the tape's contents. Auditing is an essential and exacting task. It is also tedious and can become almost hypnotizing. Rest often enough to remain alert. Do not allow yourself to be lulled into *expecting to hear* what you read.

Before beginning, be familiar with the way transcripts are prepared. Also, read any materials pertaining to the specific interview to be audited.

Work on the original copy of the transcript and correct all transcribing errors or omissions. Make all corrections in or above the lines of type. Be certain they are clearly written. Use the editing symbols given in appendix B.

While working, keep the following points in mind:

1. Be sure all words and meaningful sounds on the tape are in the transcript, that none were omitted by the transcriptionist.
2. Be sure all the words in the transcript were on the tape, that none were added by the transcriptionist.
3. Be sure the words in the transcript are the words that were spoken, that none were misunderstood and mistyped.
4. Be sure all the words are typed in the order spoken.
5. Be sure the punctuation provided by the transcriptionist conveys the speakers' intended meaning. Be cautious about changing punctuation, though, and do not change it just because you do not like the way the transcriptionist used it.
6. Try to fill in blanks which were typed because the transcriptionist could not understand what was said.
7. Correct any typographical errors.

When the auditing is finished, refile the materials used and indicate on the

INTERVIEW DATA SHEET that the transcript has been audited (see figure 11).

Figures 14 and 15 are sample audited transcript pages. Compare figure 14 with figure 12. Incorrectly transcribed words have been corrected and omitted words added. Some punctuation has been changed to more accurately reflect the sound of the interview. Figure 15 corresponds to figure 13. In addition to correcting mistranscribed words, the blanks were filled in and some punctuation and typographical errors were corrected.

Step 5: Editing

The task of the editor is to convert the audited transcript into a finished draft ready for final typing. The edited transcript must clearly convey the speakers' meanings and read smoothly enough that the reader can understand it without having to stop and reread. At the same time, the edited transcript must retain the casual quality of spoken language and the speakers' individual speech patterns. All words must be correctly spelled and the program's rules of style (appendix B) must be applied to all abbreviations, numbers, and so forth. Since the edited copy will have to be read by both the narrator and final typist, all required changes or corrections must be clearly indicated according to the program's system of editing symbols.

Be A Tolerant Critic

The verbatim transcript being edited contains all the words and meaningful sounds of the interview. Since the physical voice cannot be heard, some evidences of the speakers' individualities are missing. However, the transcript can convey an idea of personalities if it faithfully reflects the speakers' choice and arrangement of words. The transcriptionist has tried to be true to the speakers and so must you. To do that you must *be tolerant*. Think of yourself as a reader rather than an editor and consider changing only what you cannot understand at first reading. Retain improper grammar, poor sentence structure, unusual word forms, and other elements of spoken language that are not usually found in formal writing. Retain them, even if they are irritating, as long as they do not diminish clarity or impede readability.

Because the rough transcript is verbatim, it probably contains ambiguous references, awkwardly worded sentences, long run-on sentences, and fragmentary sentences. Some of these will be difficult to read or be unclear. In order to be certain that the transcript is readable and clear, *be critical*. Think of yourself now as an editor and change punctuation, delete words, insert words, and rearrange words when necessary.

To Change or Not to Change?

Grammatical errors made in casual spoken language are so common that even when they occur in written sentences one reads right over them and

Larry Mantowich (3) 142

You can have one per cent, one-tenth of one per cent of carbon monoxide, and you still have a smoldering fire. You got to have a hundred per XXX cent CO^2 before you can break that seal and start operations again.

Q: So when you seal a mine, you sometimes seal it with this cloth?

A: No, that's a ...

Q: That's just a temporary measure to get to the fire?

A: Yes. A braddish XXXX cloth is — if you had a deep room someplace and it wasn't getting enough air, you put a XXXX braddish cloth across the entry. Instead of the air going straight in, it'll turn and go into this deep room, see. ~~Just~~ Used to divert ~~the~~ air, to change ~~the~~ a current, a course of air. But I remember at Barr Coal Company where we had a fire. XXXXXXXX You know, I told you we had to seal this live mule in the mine. Well, you seal off the entire hole where the cage is at. You just board it across and trowel wood fiber or whatever it is over XX the top of this hole.

Well, you leave a pipe, a three inch pipe or any opening pipe, capped off like any other pipe. They way we did it, we had magnesium

Fig. 14. A sample audited transcript page.

Larry Mantowich (3)   145

A: Yes. And another funny thing in the mine, if a guy got on a drunk

or something, and he was in ⊙ . . . Because when you went in the mine

if you was going to load ⊙ . . . I remember when at Barr Coal Company

the _turn_ was two guys working together. They had to load

forty cars. That's twenty ton apiece. Well, they'd started sweating

from the first thing in the morning and they'd sweat until noon, and

eat dinner and then they'd sweat until quitting time again. They'd

sweat all day long. And if they was on a drunk or something,

and you could walk in that room and tha'ts all you could smell, is pure

alcohol. (laughter) Another funny thing. If you was working

beyond the last open crosscut, a little bit too far, why, they

call that working ahead of air. Well, you're working in a bottled up

place there, and you could, you'd have to leave your open light back

at the crosscut and get in there with you _coat_ first thing

in the morning and fan yourface out so you'd mix up that air becasue

that would be a pocket of gas in there. So if you'd fan it with your

coat, well, then that would mix it up with air, and then you wouldn't

light this gas. And if you didn't have very much air in your room and

Fig. 15. Another sample audited transcript page.

understands what was intended. Therefore, improper grammar should not be indiscriminately changed. "We taken the bundle" will be understood to mean "We took the bundle." "Was being a foreigner a stigmatism?" will be clear to the reader since the other speaker's response indicates understanding. "Apples is" and "we was" are clear.

False starts, repetitiveness, and crutch words are common in spoken language. Because you are working with a carefully prepared and purposely verbatim transcript, you can expect to find such elements. Consider each instance of these carefully. Listen to that part of the tape, if necessary, to determine whether these words are meaningful or whether they are habitually or nervously used. If they are meaningful, retain them; retain enough meaningless ones to reflect speech patterns.

Retain those false starts which show that a speaker did not finish a sentence because he/she thought better of it. The narrator may delete them later if he/she feels it is necessary. The following example shows a meaningful false start; the speaker started over and qualified the statement that had been begun.

> I would say yes, we were all—I would have to say I think we were all in it together. It was a group cause.

A speaker may have started a sentence and then thought of a more clear way to express the thought. Delete such a false start when all the information in it was incorporated in the new sentence. In the following example, the words "I was" should have been deleted.

> I was, I served in four or five different capacities at one time.

The following example shows how the editor inserted the information in a false start into the completed sentence. No brackets are needed to enclose insertions of this kind because the words are not really the editor's.

> On Wednesdays I took it—the dog had to go to the vet every week and I carried it there in a basket.

> The dog had to go to the vet every week and I carried it there in a basket on Wednesdays.

Repetition of a word or phrase is sometimes a meaningless false start; if so, it should be deleted. But be certain it is meaningless. In the next example the editor at first deleted the first phrase as a false start.

> Well, that goes back—my first bitter experience with John Lewis goes back to 1917.

From listening to the tape, however, it became evident that what had appeared to be a meaningless false start was actually a separate introductory sentence commonly used by storytellers. The words were put back in the transcript and the punctuation was corrected.

> Well, that goes back. My first bitter experience with John Lewis goes back to 1917.

Repetition may be a means of emphasis, of self-questioning, or of self-reassurance. If so, it should be retained and appropriately punctuated.

> It was Monday. It was Monday!
> It was Monday. It was Monday?
> It was Monday? It was Monday.

Crutch words, common in spoken language, occur frequently in transcripts. Transcriptionists were given instructions for dealing with them and were instructed to transcribe some of them; editors need to know how to handle crutch words as well. The *pauser* variety of crutch word is used unconsciously or self-consciously to fill time used for thinking. *Stammering* is a kind of pauser which should not have been transcribed. Another, *gutteral sounds*, were not transcribed if they seemed to have no meaning within the sentence. The sound Ah in the example below should not have been transcribed and would be deleted after the editor had listened to that part of the tape and ascertained that it had been used only to fill time.

Q: Ah, then when he met you, he met you in New York?

However, a gutteral sound is sometimes a meaningful indication of surprise or of sudden understanding. The Ah in the following example is correctly transcribed and should be retained by the editor.

Q: Ah, then when he met you, he met you in New York!

Gutteral sounds that indicate a speaker's, especially a narrator's, emotional or intellectual quandry should have been transcribed and should be retained. An example of a correct transcription which should be retained by the editor can be found on page 39 in Step 3: Transcribing.

Interviewer's supportive gutteral sounds, such as "mmm," "hmm" and "aha," should not have been transcribed and should be deleted if they were.

A third kind of pauser is a *habitually used word*: and, but, well, so, anyway, don't you know, you know, and like. These may occur as introductory words at the beginnings of sentences or be interjected mid-sentence. All such words should have been transcribed. However, if they are meaningless or occur too frequently, they will divert and tire the reader. Therefore, most of the meaningless ones should be deleted. Retain only enough to show that they are part of a speaker's speech pattern.

Suppose the following sentence occurred in a transcript. "Let me see, well, it was about forty years ago." If several of the narrator's pausers, such as the word "well" above, had already been retained to show individuality, then it could be deleted here to improve readability without damaging the sentence since "Let me see" indicates that the speaker was pausing to think. However, if "well" were needed in this sentence to indicate that a longer than usual pause occurred, it should be retained. You can tell whether that is the case by listening to the tape.

By all means, retain a pauser if you feel certain from the way it sounds on the tape that it is an indication of a speaker's dilemma. In the following example, the pausers were retained along with a fragmentary sentence to show that the speaker tried to avoid making an admission.

Q: Did you try to stop the argument?

A: Well, I couldn't do. . . . Well, but it wasn't, don't you know, any of my business. No. I didn't try.

The *elicitor* is the other variety of crutch word. Sometimes words such as "you know" or "see" are habitually used, but they may be meaningful requests by a speaker for assurance of understanding. If this is the case, you should retain them. That they are meaningful might be evident from context, but you might have to listen to the tape to be sure. If words are meaningful as elicitors, retain them. The preceding example shows that such an elicitor, "don't you know," was retained.

Provide Clarity

If the meaning of a sentence is ambiguous to you as a reader, it must be clarified. This is tricky business because you must *be sure* you understand the speaker's meaning. Make a change only after listening to the tape and being certain of the intended meaning.

Before inserting or rearranging words, *check the punctuation* to see if by changing it you can clarify the sentence. The following example appeared in an unedited transcript.

> I told Mr. Boardman, "You know, Mr. Smith, both of the two brothers and their father before them, had an undertaking shop right down on Fifth and Capitol."

The reader stops after Mr. Smith and thinks, "Mr. Smith? Mr. Boardman? What?" The following example shows clarifying changes in punctuation.

> I told Mr. Boardman, "You know, Mr. Smith—both of the two brothers and their father before them—had an undertaking shop right down on Fifth and Capitol."

If the punctuation seems to be all right you might need to insert, delete, or rearrange words. It is best to leave the sentence as it is, however, if after listening to the tape you are in doubt about the meaning, or if clarification would require a great deal of change. In either case, write a note to the narrator in the left margin and let him/her make the clarification.

If you decide that you can make an accurate clarification by inserting a word or two, do so, but keep such insertions to a minimum. Before making an insertion, be sure it is needed for clarification and is not an interpretive addition. Clarification is the editor's task; interpretation is the reader's task. This is sometimes a difficult distinction to make, but keep the warning in mind as you edit.

The following example shows an excerpt from an unedited transcript.

Q: Could you tell me when you first started working for the Department of Mental Health, the different institutions where you have worked, and the jobs you've held?

A: Well, when I started working, it was not known as the Department of Mental Health, Public Safety. The best I can remember, it was 1941, Illinois Security Hospital.

The editor made the following insertions, some needed, some not.

A: Well, when I started working, it was not known as the Department of Mental Health, [but as] Public Safety. The best I can remember, [my first job] was 1941 [with the] Illinois Security Hospital.

The first insertion [but as] is necessary because on the tape it was evident that Public Safety was not spoken of as a division of the Department of Mental Health as the comma alone might imply. The second insertion [my first job] is actually a rewording. It was made to clarify what the editor considered an unclear reference to the pronoun "it." This second insertion is unnecessary because the inserted words can be understood from the question. A more accurate insertion, if one were necessary, might have been [the year I first started working]. The third insertion [with the] is probably also unnecessary because those words can also be understood from the question. In fact, the interviewer's next question brought forth a clarification and amplification of this part of the answer.

When clarifying insertions are made, it is necessary to place some of them within brackets so users will know that they are the editor's words and not the speaker's. Bracket a pronoun's antecedent inserted to clarify an ambiguous reference. After listening to the tape, the editor made and bracketed the needed clarifying insertions in the following sentences:

They were along on the north side of the square and he was a few paces ahead of Mrs. Chin and Mr. Miller, and he [Mr. Miller] was making Mrs. Chin understand they were not going home with this much more money.

We had practically an acre in the front yard, and not a motor-driven lawn mower; it [the mower's motive power] was ours.

Bracket major verbs. Forms of the verb "to be" are commonly unspoken but understood in conversation; if you decide such verbs need to be inserted, they need no brackets. The first sentence in the following example is unclear to the reader and the narrator did not make its meaning clear until three sentences later.

We were on this strike fighting against an imposition that the coal company had imposed upon us where the loaders would add their loads 275 more pounds for the ton. . . . (Two sentences have been deleted to shorten this example.) In other words, the loader had to load 2,275 pounds of coal to get paid for the ton, and we were on strike to remove that imposition.

As shown in the next example, in order to clarify that first sentence, a verb form was changed with the insertion of [have to] and the preposition "to" was inserted after "add."

We were on this strike fighting against an imposition that the coal company had imposed upon us where the loaders would [have to] add to their loads 275 more pounds for the ton.

It is usually not necessary to bracket inserted prepositions (see the inserted "to" in the example above), conjunctions, or articles.

Provide Readability

Essentially clear but awkwardly worded sentences will need to be made easier to read. If you stumble when reading a sentence, read it more carefully a second time. If it is still difficult to understand, listen to the tape to find a way to make the sentence read more easily. It may be possible to change the punctuation to better reflect the speaker's emphasis. It may be necessary to rearrange parts of a sentence: a grammar book will help you rearrange words with the least change necessary. No matter what change is made, be sure not to change the speaker's meaning. Brackets are not used when a speaker's words or phrases are rearranged.

Running one thought into the next with conjunctions is a habit of some speakers. It may be helpful to the reader to divide the longest, most unwieldy of such sentences. However, do not change so many that the reader is left unaware of this habit.

The following, from a rough transcript, is a good example of a run-on sentence:

> One of our directors had interests in Texas and he was there on business, and he went to church and when he came home he called his wife and he said he had been so happy to go to the church but there was a family that was in the deepest sorrow because of a son who had run away from home, and we were praying for that child.

The edited sentence is shown in the example below. A run-on sentence was divided. Also, after listening to the tape, the editor added quotation marks to the last clause because they were indicated by the speaker's tone of voice. The omission of quotation marks was a transcribing error and should have been corrected during auditing. With their insertion, both the clarity of the sentence and its readability are improved.

> One of our directors had interests in Texas and he was there on business, and he went to church. When he came home he called his wife and he said he had been so happy to go to the church but there was a family that was in the deepest sorrow because of a son who had run away from home and, "We were praying for that child."

When a transcript is composed mainly of short and choppy or incomplete sentences, the reader may have trouble following or concentrating on otherwise useful information. Listen to the tape to see if these really reflect a speaker's style. They may, because some people speak that way. If they were correctly transcribed, leave them as they are.

If listening to the tape shows that the transcript reflects the transcriptionist's rather than the speaker's style, repunctuation is in order. What appear as sentences may really be clauses or phrases separated by pauses which were mistaken for the ends of sentences. If so, combine these and repunctuate to show there were pauses. Be sure that the combining creates a sentence that reflects the speaker's intended meaning.

The following example shows a series of mistranscribed short sentences.

> The house stood on the hill. And beside it was the old house. And down the hill behind was the barn. A red barn with a calf shed attached. And next to that the hog pen.

The following is an example of combining and repunctuating of the above. "And" introducing the last sentence was deleted because it was a meaningless diversion to the reader and examples of its use had been retained in previous sentences.

> The house stood on the hill, and beside it was the old house. And down the hill behind was the barn—a red barn with a calf shed attached. Next to that was the hog pen.

Fragmentary sentences are common in speech and in transcripts. Retain them when they can be understood. In the following example, the second "sentence" is clear enough to retain.

> We're doing basically the same thing that we always did. Only on a smaller scale. So this is how you're affected.

If the meaning of a fragmentary sentence is not clear, combine it with an adjacent sentence or make an insertion to complete it. The following example from an unedited transcript is verbatim, is punctuated fairly well, reflects the way the words were said by the narrator, but is unclear.

> It was established there as that was the Levee in those days and that was the place where the most people were who were anxiously needing a place of refuge, and they considered it that. And came readily, and it grew so that the first building was short for they outgrew it.

It was apparent from the tape that the speaker's breath usually gave out before her thought was completely expressed. When she had to stop for breath she did, and the transcriptionist ended the sentence. Refreshed, the narrator went right on with her thought and in doing so she omitted the subject of the first clause of the transcriptionist's next sentence. The listener could follow, but the reader has trouble.

The editor changed punctuation, deleted a conjunction, and moved the misplaced clause to the first sentence. This clarified the second sentence, made it more readable, and retained the speaker's style. The second sentence still seemed ambiguous, so the insertions were made.

> It was established there as that was the Levee in those days, and that was the place where the most people were who were anxiously needing a place of refuge; they considered it that and came readily. And it grew so that the first building was [used only a] short [time] for they outgrew it.

Don't make a change simply for the sake of proper sentence structure. Change a sentence only to make it easier to read. The transcriptionist took pains to type what was said the way it was said. Be as careful to retain as much of the original transcript as possible. The following example shows a verbatim sentence and then the same sentence after the editor had unnecessarily rearranged words.

> And do you know, people from all over this country, I've gotten letters from everywhere, telling me what he had meant to them.

> And do you know, I've gotten letters from everywhere, from people all over this country, telling me what he had meant to them.

The problem with the verbatim sentence is only that the narrator changed construction mid-sentence; that can be solved by changing punctuation to more accurately reflect the sound on the tape as in the example below.

> And do you know, people from all over this country—I've gotten letters from everywhere telling me what he had meant to them.

An interviewer's awkward question may need to be reworded, but be sure the narrator's answer still follows from it.

The Unspoken Message

A speaker's emphatic pauses, inflection and tone of voice, and expressions of emotion are as much a part of his/her message as are the words. When a transcription is made, this part of the message can be lost unless an effort is made to reflect these elements of speech in the transcript.

Pauses, inflection, and tone of voice can be conveyed to some extent through punctuation. Use punctuation as you learned to use it as a writer and reader. A comma, for example, means "pause here" or "watch out now, this is a little different." In transcripts, commas can also be used to imply a certain length of pause or degree of difference—the shortest pause and the least difference. The dash, two hyphens typed together, means a slightly longer pause and a greater degree of difference. The three points of the ellipsis, when they occur within a sentence or after a period, indicate a much longer pause but should be used sparingly and appropriately. (See the rules of style, appendix B.)

In the following example, all these elements of punctuation were used to reflect sound as well as meaning, and to convey an especailly choppy narrative.

> Cousin Lou, she ran to hide. And I—being the oldest one there—I gave, I think it was, three guns . . . let's see, Ed and Bess and I had one, and I gave. . . . Yes, four guns. So I gave each one a gun and I said, "Now, when I tell the youngest to open the door," I says, "when I say shoot—shoot."

Inflection and tone of voice can be conveyed through the use of the exclamation point, but be careful not to use it so frequently that it loses its impact upon the reader. If underlining is used in this way, its use should also be kept to a minimum.

Audible expressions of emotion and action have been included in the transcript and placed in parentheses: (laughs), (weeps), (pounds fist on table), (tape turned off and on again). Laughter, like a crutch word, may be a nervous habit. If many instances of seemingly inappropriate laughter are found in the transcript, listen to those sections. If it is nervous laughter, retain only enough instances to show the speaker's habit.

The preceding pages have explained how it is possible, by being both tolerant and critical, to prepare a clear and easy-to-read transcript that retains the casual quality of spoken language and the speaker's individualities. You can refer to them again in solving editing problems. The following pages will help you to be sure that details such as spelling and printing style are correct. The final pages contain a brief list of instructions for editors.

Be Correct

All words in the edited transcript must be spelled correctly and, if there is more than one accepted spelling, consistently. The editor has final responsibility for this. Use a dictionary whenever a word looks peculiar or you are not certain of its spelling. The transcript should contain common contractions if the speakers used them, but not ones which were invented to convey dialect. "Can't" and "would've" are acceptable, but "comin'n'goin' " and "more'n' enuf" are not. Words pronounced in a careless or colloquial way should be correctly spelled. Type "get," not "git," and "running," not "runnin'."

A rare exception to using correct spelling is made for consistently mispronounced significant words. The transcriptionist might have deliberately misspelled a mispronounced word if it seemed important to do so, but should have made a note of such misspellings in the left margin. Watch for such notes and decide whether to retain those misspellings and explain them in footnotes or to correct them. Remember that retained misspellings should have real significance.

For example, as mentioned earlier, if a speaker consistently used the colloquial pronunciation "Meredosh" for Meredosia, an Illinois town, and the transcriptionist typed it and made a note of it, it can be retained by inserting the correct spelling after it, within brackets, at each occurrence. At the first occurrence, write a footnote briefly explaining what has been done. Another method of indicating to the reader that this pronunciation was consistently used is by correcting the misspelling at each occurrence, but at the first occurrence writing a footnote containing that information.

In the editorial function of ascertaining the correct spelling of all words, you may find that the transcriptionist typed such a mispronunciation without realizing it was incorrect. In this case it would be necessary to make the same kind of decision about retention or correction of that misspelling.

Make a word list for your own convenience. The interviewer, with the help of the narrator, should have prepared a word list as an aid for the transcriptionist, who is expected to sit and type. As editor, do research, if necessary, to ascertain spelling and do not rely on the accuracy of that word list. Making your own list will simplify your task. (See the sample in figure 16.)

Include on this list all technical or colloquial terms, all names of people and places, the spellings preferred for variously spelled words, the form to be used for compound words (whether hyphenated or not), and abbreviations. The first time such a word occurs in the transcript, try to verify it or decide on its form immediately.

Verify spellings of names by checking them in a phone directory, *Who's Who,* or other available sources. Place names can be verified by consulting an

Word List -- Tobias Williams Memoir

Verified	Word, Abbrev., etc.	Pg. of first occurrence	Also on pgs.	Corrected
✓	Evan MacDonald	1	2, 5, 6, 9, 13	ok.
✓	Sisser, Illinois	1	4, 5,	✓
✓	PMWA [Progressive Mine Workers of America] (Qs? NO)	2	3, 4, 5, 7, 11, 12,	ok
✓	John L. Lewis	2	4, 5, 8, 9,	ok
✓	black-damp	3		✓
✓	judgement	3	4,	✓
	percent not per cent	4	11, 12, 14	ok
	central Illinois not Central	4	7, 8, 11, 13	ok

Fig. 16. A sample word list.

atlas, gazetteer, or state map. The spellings of technical and foreign words, colloquial terms, and professional jargon should be verified by consulting a book on the particular subject or a specialized reference work.

If a name is spelled correctly or a word or abbreviation appears in the rough transcript in the form desired for the final transcript, write it on the list as it is at that first occurrence and check "verified" and "corrected." Record the page number of first occurrence. When it occurs again, verify or change it by looking at the word list. Record the page number on which the word "also occurs."

If you can't immediately verify or decide, write the word on the list as it appears at its first occurrence in the transcript; record the page number of the first and each following occurrence. If the spelling or form is different in later occurrences, make note of that by circling that page number. When finished with the initial editing, do the required research. If you find a word is correct on the list, check "verified" and "corrected." If not, correct it on the list.

When you have verified everything possible, make necessary changes in the transcript. Be sure to correct each occurrence on all pages indicated on the list. When this is done, check "corrected." File the list with the transcript when finished editing. You may not be able to verify all words. If not, be sure unverified words are brought to the attention of the narrator. He/she may be able to verify or correct them or offer some clues for further work. Use the filed word list as an aid in making all corrections after the narrator's review.

Apply the Rules of Style

Part of the editor's task is to make sure that the transcript follows the program's rules of style. These rules outline ways to express abbreviations and numbers, to amplify abbreviations and names, and to use capitalization and punctuation. Appendix B of this manual is a compilation of such rules. Users will find an oral history transcript easier to read when it follows recognized or at least consistent and understandable standards of style. The speaker's meaning can be clouded by an editor's sloppy attention to those details. Keep a copy of the rules handy as a reference; you will need to use it often.

Because the rules cover only the most commonly encountered problems, it may be necessary to consult a book on style or grammar to find ways to handle some details. Sometimes such resources are not helpful because they are designed primarily for use with formal, written language and an oral history transcript derives from the spoken word. For that reason, novels with plenty of dialogue or a book based on oral history interviews might prove to be good resources. If an answer is difficult to find, consult with co-workers and use your own judgment to solve the problem. In deciding on a solution, try to follow the existing rules as closely as possible so that the means of expression chosen will be recognizable and immediately understandable to the reader. For easy future reference, make a note of the problem and solution in a copy of the rules and share it with co-workers.

Be Consistent

Apply the rules of style consistently in similar situations throughout the transcript. At every instance of a word or number that needs to be changed, indicate the change in the transcript. For example, the final typist should not be expected to remember to change "McBride" to "MacBride" or know to change "40" to "forty" if that is not indicated at each occurrence.

Be Neat

Use the program's list of editing symbols (a sample is included in appendix B) and make all corrections and changes clearly. Make them in or above the lines of type.

The kind of pen/pencil to use is a matter debated by editors. Unless one is an extremely neat, precise, and decisive person, using an erasable pencil is probably best. Whether using pen or pencil, be sure it has a fine enough point to allow for writing clearly. Felt tip pens are not good to use with cheap, absorbent paper.

The color to use is another matter to decide. Some people object to using red on copy the narrator will review because it seems too critical, too much like the teacher's red checks on a spelling test. Others use it because it makes corrections obvious. Some programs circle or underline blanks and questioned sections with a second color so that the narrator will take special note during his/her review. If this is done, the final typist should of course be told what those colors mean.

A Second Reading

When the transcript has been edited for clarity, readability, and correct handling of details, you will need to start again. This time read it through to ascertain semantic flow. You want to be sure it reads smoothly and clearly, but there may be additional errors in spelling and style as well. As you read, do not assume that the transcript reads well simply because of your familiarity with its content. Be critical of your own work. Because this is difficult, some programs ask the interviewer or another staff person to perform this reading. The reader should make a list of the lines and pages on which further work is needed. If a person other than the editor does this reading, it should be kept in mind that editors' styles differ. If you disagree with the way something was done, be tolerant. But if a sentence does not read well or is unclear, or if there are instances where similar situations are handled very differently, make note. The original editor should make the needed changes.

Editing Instructions

When checking out a transcript to edit, indicate the date work began on the INTERVIEW DATA SHEET. Keep a cumulative record of the time spent and attach it to the transcript. When finished, record that total time on the INTERVIEW DATA SHEET (see figure 11).

Before beginning, learn how a transcript is prepared. Read the INTERVIEWER'S COMMENTS and INTERVIEW CONTENTS pertaining to the specific transcript to be edited. Be sure not to misplace any of these items; they are primary historical documents which cannot be replaced.

If you were assigned to do the auditing as well as the editing, you will have heard the tape. If not, listen to enough of it to get the feel of the interview—to become familiar with the speech patterns and mannerisms of the speakers—and to learn how the transcriptionist used punctuation. Refer to the tape as frequently as necessary to avoid destroying clarity, misconstruing meaning, or diminishing individuality.

When you edit, you will be making certain that (1) meaningless false starts and crutch words have been deleted often enough for readability but not so often that the speaker's individuality has disappeared; (2) formerly ambiguous and unclear sentences have been accurately clarified or marked for the narrator to improve; (3) formerly awkward sentences no longer impede reading but still reflect the speaker's intended meaning or are marked; (4) punctuation is used sparingly enough for readability but accurately reflects what was said the way it was said; (5) all spelling is accurate, appropriate, and consistent or is marked for the narrator to verify; and (6) the rules of style have been applied accurately and consistently.

When you think you have accomplished the six items listed above, then you are ready to begin the second reading to be sure the transcript has semantic flow. If you find spots that need more work, list them by line and page number so that you can work on them when you finish the second reading.

When you are finished with the transcript, file it and any materials used, and record the total time on the INTERVIEW DATA SHEET.

Figures 17 and 18 show edited transcript pages corresponding to the audited pages shown in figures 14 and 15, respectively. Compare them to see what editing was done to each.

Step 6: Finishing Touches

Narrator's Review

When the transcript is edited, it is ready for review by the narrator. The object of the review is to ascertain that the transcript reflects the narrator's intended meaning and that the facts are presented the way the narrator wants them to stand. Some programs have the edited transcript retyped so that the narrator can work with clean copy, but this is not necessary if transcribing, auditing, and editing were done carefully.

Some narrators are fully capable of carrying out the review on their own. If you feel that, given a narrator's health, age, education, and experience, he/she will be able to understand the directions and carry them through effectively, then you might ask that the review be done independently. This is helpful, especially with long memoirs that would require a staff member's making several visits to assist with review. The transcript can be taken or mailed to the narrator.

With narrators who live near enough to the office that transcripts can be taken, this is the preferred method. The editor is the ideal person to deliver the transcript and explain what needs to be done because he/she is the most knowledgeable about it. The interviewer could do it, especially when there is reason to believe that the narrator might be more cooperative that way. If the interviewer takes the transcript, the editor should explain any special problems before it is delivered. If it is the policy to have editors deliver transcripts, it is helpful to have the interviewer tell the narrator at their last meeting that someone else will contact him/her about the review, and a nice touch to have the interviewer go along at least to make introductions.

Make an appointment with the narrator, and state that you will bring the transcript and explain the reviewing task. Take along a copy of the PROOF-READING INSTRUCTIONS FOR NARRATORS (see figure 19) to use to explain the purpose of the review, how to approach it, and how to carry it through. Explain the program's editing symbols so that the narrator can use them in mak-

Larry Mantowich (3)   142

You can have ~~one~~ per cent, ~~one-tenth~~ $1/10$ of ~~one~~ per cent of carbon monox-

ide, and you still have a smoldering fire. You got to have ~~a hundred~~ 100

per ~~XXX~~ cent CO^2 before you can break that seal and start operation

again.

Q: So when you seal a mine, you sometimes seal it with this cloth?

A: No, that's a ...

Q: That's just a temporary measure to get to the fire?

A: Yes. A braddish[brattice], ~~XXXX~~ cloth is —— if you had a deep room some-

place and it wasn't getting enough air, you put a ~~XXXX~~ braddish[brattice] cloth

across the entry. Instead of the air going straight in, it'll turn

and go into this deep room, see. ~~Just~~ Used to divert ~~the~~ air, change ~~the~~ to a

current, a course of air. But I remember at Barr Coal Company where we

had a fire. ~~XXXXXXXXX~~ You know, I told you we had to seal this live

mule in the mine. Well, you seal off the entire hole where the cage

is at. You just board it across and trowel wood fiber or whatever

it is over ~~IX~~ the top of this hole.

No

Well, you leave a pipe, a three inch pipe or any opening pipe, capped

off like any other pipe. They way we did it, we had magnesium

[brattice]: Braddish will appear throughout the transcript, as the narrator consistently mispronounced the word brattice in that way. A brattice is a partition, especially one erected in a mine for ventilation. (Ed.)

Fig. 17. Sample edited transcript page.

Larry Mantowich (3)   145

A: Yes. And another funny thing in the mine, if a guy got on a drunk

or something, and he was in ⊘ . . . Because when you went in the mine,

if you was going to load ⊙___ I remember when at Barr Coal Company

the _turn_ was two guys working together. They had to load

forty cars. That's twenty ton apiece. Well, they'd started sweating

from the first thing in the morning and they'd sweat until noon, and

eat dinner, and then they'd sweat until quitting time again. They'd

sweat all day long. And if they was on a drunk or something, and

and you could walk in that room and tha'ts all you could smell, is pure

alcohol. (laughter) Another funny thing. If you was working the

beyond the last open crosscut, a little bit too far, why, they

called that working ahead of air. Well, you're working in a bottled up

place there, and you could you'd have to leave your open light back

at the crosscut and get in there with your ___coat___ first thing

in the morning and fan your face out so you'd mix up that air, because

that would be a pocket of gas in there. So if you'd fan it with your

coat, well, then that would mix it up with air, and then you wouldn't

light this gas. And if you didn't have very much air in your room and

Fig. 18. Another edited transcript page.

vicinity to help with the review. Mail the transcript to that person, including full instructions. Write a letter to the narrator explaining that someone will be contacting him/her about the review.

Write the date on which the transcript was taken or mailed on the INTER-VIEW DATA SHEET. Check the "Returned" column when you have finished helping with the review or the transcript has been returned by mail (see figure 11). If it is not returned by the deadline set or within what the program considers a reasonable time, send a gentle reminder, followed by a stronger but understanding letter. If these produce no results, make a phone call asking when the transcript may be picked up. If there is still no response on transcripts mailed to distant persons or if a narrator puts you off, inform the narrator of a deadline date after which it will be assumed that the unreturned transcript meets the narrator's approval and final processing will move ahead. If a large number of transcripts are out for review, you might want to set up a dated file of cards for keeping records straight.

Final Reading and Reediting

When the reviewed transcript is returned to the office, the editor should reread it to be sure clarity and readability have been maintained and that all changes, deletions, additions, and explanations will be clear to the final typist. Make spelling changes indicated by the narrator at each occurrence throughout the transcript.

If there are still some blanks in the transcript, something must be done to clarify the text or explain the gaps to readers. When only one or two words are missing and they do not seem to make an appreciable difference to the meaning of a sentence, there is no need to indicate their absence. Simply make a note to the final typist to ignore the blanks and close up the space. If a blank accounts for important words which can be supplied by approximation from context, do so. Place the inserted words in brackets.

The word inaudible raises suspicions these days, but it may have to be used. Longer sections left blank will have to be explained. The following example shows blanks left in a reviewed transcript.

> We children _____
> _____ milk-
> ing. _____
> to town at once. We needed no coaxing, because we saw our cousins there and
> had a great time.

The following example shows that during reediting the editor made a guess based on the context of the missing material and inserted the words in brackets.

> We children [helped with the] milking. [Then we all went] to town at once.[1]
> We needed no coaxing because we saw our cousins there and had a great time.

The numeral one in the above example indicates an explanatory footnote would be placed at the bottom of the transcript page. It might read, "This is an approximation of at least two partially inaudible sentences. (Ed.)"

The next example shows how to handle longer inaudible sections.

> We children [. . .][2]
> We needed no coaxing, because we
> saw our cousins and had a great time.

The explanatory footnote for this example might read, "Approximately eighteen minutes of the interview were made inaudible by electrical interference. (Ed.)"

When you have completed rereading, check that column on the INTERVIEW DATA SHEET (see figure 11).

The Preface

A preface needs to be written some time before final typing is completed. The writing of the preface can be done by any staff person, but the interviewer probably is best qualified. He/she is familiar with the interview and might have biographical information that no one else has. A transcriptionist or editor could prepare the preface because of their familiarity with the interview. If some other person is asked to do it, the writing could be done after reading the transcript, the INTERVIEWER'S COMMENTS and the INTERVIEW DATA SHEET. Indicate completion of the preface on the INTERVIEW DATA SHEET.

The preface to an oral history memoir has a two-fold purpose. First, in two or three paragraphs it should introduce the reader to the narrator, establish the narrator's "credentials," and tell the reader why he/she should be interested in this particular memoir. Secondly, the preface must include some basic information about oral history. It should contain a standardized introductory paragraph giving identifying information—who was interviewed by whom and when, and the names of the transcriptionist and editor. This is followed by one or two paragraphs of biographical information including place and date of birth, schooling, occupation, activities, and so forth. It should also establish the narrator's expertise in discussing a particular topic. This part of the preface may be two or three paragraphs long depending on the experiences of the narrator. It should be no longer, as its purpose is only to entice the reader.

The first of two concluding paragraphs explains that it is a transcript of the spoken word; that all involved in its preparation tried to preserve the informal, conversational style inherent in such historical sources; and that the sponsoring institution is not responsible for factual accuracy. The second of these paragraphs states the conditions of use to which the transcript can be put. A sample preface is shown in figure 21.

Final typists should be provided with specific instructions on how to set up and paginate the preface pages.

The Title Page

The title page can be prepared at the same time as the preface. It should contain the title of the memoir, the title of the project of which it is a part if that applies, and copyright information. Figure 22 shows a sample title page. Instruct the final typist on the format for this page.

Final Typing

By the time the final typist receives the transcript it should be in correct form. If there are questions about what to do or if something seems wrong, the typist should ask the editor for clarification. If something is not clear, it may not be clear to the reader either, so it should be brought to the editor's attention. Changes should not be made without talking to the editor because there is probably a good reason for the way the transcript appears.

PREFACE

This manuscript is the product of a tape-recorded interview conducted by Rex Rhodes for the Oral History Office, Sangamon State University in November, 1972. Betty Kyger transcribed the tape and Dan Horton edited the transcript.

Mr. Small was born in Harrisburg, Illinois, in 1904. As a teenager he began a career in journalism that spans more than half a century. In 1931, at the time of serious coal mining troubles and union rivalries, he became general manager and editor of the Harrisburg Daily Register. From that vantage point he observed and reported many of the major incidents in the mine wars of central and southern Illinois.

Readers of this oral history memoir should bear in mind that it is a transcript of the spoken word, and that the interviewer, narrator and editor sought to preserve the informal, conversational style that is inherent in such historical sources. Sangamon State University is not responsible for the factual accuracy of the memoir, nor for views expressed therein; these are for the reader to judge.

The manuscript may be read, quoted and cited freely. It may not be reproduced in whole or in part by any means, electronic or mechanical, without written permission in writing from the Oral History Office, Sangamon State Univeristy, Springfield, Illinois, 62708.

Fig. 21. A sample preface.

One needs to understand exactly what is being typed in order to type intelligently. Therefore, one must understand how transcribing and editing were done and be familiar with the program's rules of style and the editing symbols. Complete typing specifications should be provided. These cover margins, spacing, paragraphing, the use of brackets [ ] and parentheses ( ), and instructions for typing footnotes, preface, and title page specifications. Any special instructions for a particular transcript should have been written by the editor and explained.

Write the date final typing is begun on the INTERVIEW DATA SHEET. Check the Text Finished column when the text and preface have been typed.

Proofreading

A memoir which has been typed in final form should next be proofread against the edited copy of the transcript. This is best done by two people working together. One person reads the edited copy aloud, even the punctuation, unusual word forms, and the spellings of proper names. The second person should follow along in the final typed copy. He/she should read carefully and concentrate on each word, checking for typing errors and also for still possible spelling errors. All errors found in the final typed copy should be listed on a

ARTHUR BRITTIN MEMOIR

Springfield Race Riot Project

Fig. 22. The title page.

separate sheet of paper by page numbers, line numbers, and changes to be made.

When proofread, the transcript and the list of changes should be given to the final typist so corrections can be made. Indicate completion of these steps on the INTERVIEW DATA SHEET.

Preparing the Table of Contents and Index

Before duplicating and binding the final copy is an ideal time to prepare a table of contents and an index for each memoir. Some oral history offices ask their transcriptionists to prepare preliminary indexes as they work with the interview. But it is only when the transcript pages have been given final pagination that these two finder's aids can be completed. It is probably wiser and less time-consuming to have one staff person act as indexer and compile the tables of contents and indexes directly from the final copy. Exact procedures for these tasks are discussed under Step 7: Serving Users. Upon completion of a table of contents or index, check the appropriate boxes on the INTERVIEW DATA SHEET.

Tables of contents and indexes are not really essential parts of the finished oral history product, but they are valuable and fairly simple ways to make material accessible. If office personnel is limited and a long period of time is foreseen before indexing can be implemented, it is best to go ahead and copy and bind the memoirs now. The highest priority should remain getting the tape transcribed, typed in readable form, and shelved as quickly as possible. A table of contents and/or index can always be added to the text at some later date as resources allow. If the program has serious intentions of indexing memoirs in the future, a temporary system of looseleaf binding will probably be a wise investment.

Collateral Materials

Another decision which should be made at this time involves collateral material. Many programs include at least a picture of the narrator in the finished manuscript, often as a frontispiece. If it is decided that other pictures, newspaper articles, or other illustrative material should also be included with the final copy, their format and position within the text should be considered now.

Many programs prefer to shelve their collateral material separately from their memoirs, though a memoir's impact can be greatly enhanced by combining the two. It is often feasible, if the amount of collateral material is not large, to provide space for it in a pocket within a memoir's back cover, if bound, or inside a loose-leaf binder. If such collaterals are filed separately, be sure to institute some sort of shelving or cataloging arrangement for them so that patrons will be aware of their existence and find them easily accessible.

How Many Final Copies?

The number of final copies needed of each memoir will depend on the financial resources of the program as well as the extent of the dissemination efforts. It is customary to send a complimentary copy to each narrator as a way of thanking him/her for consenting to be interviewed and participating in the oral history program.

A second copy should be made to be shelved in the oral history office and used by patrons. Some programs also make an extra copy for this purpose in case of theft, loss, or heavy usage.

Your program may have agreed to deposit duplicates of your holdings in a state or historical library, or another oral history center which acts as a central repository for oral history materials. Such a setup can be of great assistance in making memoirs widely accessible. Prepare extra copies needed for this purpose.

One final copy should be made, but not bound, if one is considering the possibility of contracting with Microfilming Corporation of America to have the collection made available on microfiche. This will be discussed in more detail under Step 8: Reaching the Public. The decision should be made early on so that there will be an extra copy of each transcript when you are ready to mail.

What Kind of Final Copies?

Once the number of copies needed has been calculated, decide on the means of duplication to be used. Both photocopy and offset printing can be done directly from a typed transcript. Offset printing is likely to be more expensive, but produces better copy. Typeset printing is quite expensive, but is more formal, more bookish in appearance. The answer to this question depends almost entirely on your financial resources and the value your program places on a professional appearance for your memoirs.

A second issue which must be decided is how the memoirs will be bound. Least expensive and most flexible is the loose-leaf binder. As discussed previously, if the number of finishing touches which can be applied to a transcript is really limited at this time, loose-leaf may be the best choice. Further processing steps can always be added at a later date. But there is the problem of losing pages, giving such a binder system little permanency.

Spiral binding is a bit better, as pages can not so easily come out. This method is nearly as economical as loose-leaf binding, and does permit the addition of more pages, such as an index or table of contents, if necessary. Adhesive binding is more permanent and more resembles a book. But pages still are not secure with this method unless it is meticulously done, and the appearance of the memoir will not be good unless some sort of covers and binding tape are used. Stitch binding and buckram covers entail considerable expense, but give the finished product a polished look. Such a binding will take a lot of use and not require the special handling or repair of less expensive methods.

When the number of copies needed has been determined, and the method of binding, send them to be duplicated and bound. Indicate the date they were sent and that they have been returned on the INTERVIEW DATA SHEET. Shelve the office copy and distribute the others, checking that such has been done on the INTERVIEW DATA SHEET.

Figures 23 and 24 are sample final transcript pages. Compare them with figures 17 and 18 respectively.

Larry Mantowich   120

You can have 1 per cent, 1/10 of 1 per cent of carbon monoxide, and you still have a smoldering fire. You got to have 100 per cent CO^2 before you can break that seal and start operation again.

Q: So when you seal a mine, you sometimes seal it with this cloth?

A: No, that's a . . .

Q: That's just a temporary measure to get to the fire?

A: Yes. A braddish [brattice][1] cloth is--if you had a deep room some-place and it wasn't getting enough air, you put a braddish [brattice] cloth across the entry. Instead of the air going straight in, it'll turn and go into this deep room, see. Used to divert air, to change a current, a course of air. But I remember at Barr Coal Company where we had a fire. You know, I told you we had to seal this live mule in the mine. Well, you seal off the entire hole where the cage is at. You just board it across and trowel wood fiber or whatever it is over the top of this hole. Well, you leave a pipe, a three-inch pipe or any opening pipe, capped off like any other pipe. The way we did it, we had magnesia bottles.

Q: Milk of magnesia bottles?

A: Yes, yes. That's right. Because it had a little cap. Remember a cap years ago when they had little wires on it? You could cap that off right away. Well, that's the way that was. So we'd fill this magnesia

---

[1]Braddish will appear throughout the transcript as the narrator consistently mispronounced the word brattice in that way. A brattice is a partition, especially one erected in a mine for ventilation. Ed.

Fig. 23. Final transcript page containing the edited transcript page shown in figure 17.

EXERCISE 4: TRANSCRIBING A PRACTICE MEMOIR

Following the transcribing guidelines and typing instructions and specifications in Step 3: Transcribing, transcribe the tape recording made in Exercise 3. Try to reproduce on paper the words, sounds, emotion, and action heard on the tape.

EXERCISE 5: AUDITING A PRACTICE MEMOIR

Following the guidelines and instructions in Step 4: Auditing, audit the transcript made in Exercise 4. Proofread the transcript from the tape, correcting any errors made in transcribing.

Larry Mantowich   122

A: Yes. And another funny thing in the mine, if a guy got on a drunk or something, and he was in. . . . Because when you went in the mine, if you was going to load--I remember when at Barr Coal Company the turn was two guys working together. They had to load forty cars. That's twenty ton apiece. Well, they'd start sweating from the first thing in the morning and they'd sweat until noon, cut dinner, and then they'd sweat until quitting time agin. They'd sweat all day long. And if they was on a drunk or something, you could walk in that room and that's all you could smell is pure alcohol. (laughter)

Another funny thing. If you was working beyond the last open crosscut, a little bit too far, why, they called that working ahead of air. Well, you're working in a bottled up place there, and you'd have to leave your open light back at the crosscut and get in there with your coat first thing in the morning and fan your face out so you'd mix up that air, because that would be a pocket of gas in there. So if you'd fan it with your coat, well, then that would mix it up with air, and then you wouldn't light this gas. And if you didn't have very much air in your room and the mule driver would come in and pull your car, that mule would drink up your air about five times faster than a man, you know. (laughter) He'd just about drink up all that air that you had in there, just by pulling this one car. (laughter)

Q: So what do you do? Fan some more when the mule's gone?

A: No, because you're active. You're shoveling and everything. That

Fig. 24. Final transcript page showing how the edited page in figure 18 looks when retyped.

EXERCISE 6: EDITING A PRACTICE MEMOIR

Edit the transcript audited in Exercise 5; follow the guidelines and instructions in Step 5: Editing, and use the rules of style and editing symbols given in appendix B. Remember to be a tolerant critic and try to be true to the speakers as you prepare a transcript readers can read easily and understand.

EXERCISE 7: APPLYING THE FINISHING TOUCHES

Following the guidelines in Step 6: Finishing Touches, perform the following tasks:

(a) Take or send the edited transcript to the narrator for review. Explain what the reviewing task is for and what it involves on the narrator's part.

(b) Upon receiving the reviewed transcript, reread it to be certain readability has not been diminished by any changes made by the narrator.

(c) Prepare a preface for the memoir which informs the reader and is an inducement to read the memoir. Write the last two paragraphs to fit your own situation.

IV

Disseminating Oral History

C ollecting and processing oral history is a vital and a gratifying experience. But a cabinet of tapes and a shelf of transcripts are only a stock of curiosities unless patrons—both actual and potential— know that the collection exists, know what it contains, and know how to gain access to its information. Only with such dissemination and accessibility can the collection be considered historical resource material.

Disseminating oral history to the public consists of (1) serving actual users by producing such customary finder's aids as an index, table of contents, and a card catalog of memoirs; and (2) reaching the public by providing information about the collection in reference and bibliographic works, placing the collection within convenient reach of potential users, and publicizing its availability.

Step 7: Serving Users

Having prepared the transcripts in final form, it is tempting to feel that the job is done. Taped for history are a series of interviews with people whose historical information might otherwise have gone unrecorded. That in itself is important, but the collection of memoirs is useless unless those who need the information can find it. Concern about accessibility can be partly alleviated by providing a comprehensive retrieval system.

Providing a retrieval system is a three-part process consisting of:

1. the indexing of interview (tape) contents
2. indexing of transcripts
3. assembling a card catalog for an entire oral history collection.

Each of these may stand alone as a finder's aid, but used in conjunction with the others, provides a comprehensive system of retrieval which most facilitates the researcher's/user's task.

Many oral history programs feel that the more concise and detailed the retrieval system, the greater the number of people who will be encouraged to use their oral history material. And that, for them, is the reward in all of this—greater ease of accessibility. Researchers are not prone to go out of their way to investigate material that they cannot at least quickly determine to be of some value to their work. Therefore, to save oral history material from gathering dust and to encourage researchers to use this still somewhat unconventional source of historical information, every attempt must be made to make it as available and easy to use as more conventional resources.

Indexing Tapes

The first of this three-part system is the indexing of the tapes themselves on the INTERVIEW CONTENTS sheet. This was previously discussed in detail in Step 2. Composed by the interviewer as immediately after the interview as possible, the INTERVIEW CONTENTS sheet is indispensable for any oral history program. Because the INTERVIEW CONTENTS descriptions are accompanied by indications of tape time, it is possible to get a helpful perspective on the interview—what major topics and important names are mentioned. Some programs, because of budget and personnel limitations, may have to be content with having the tape as the finished product. For them, this INTERVIEW CONTENTS sheet would be a satisfactory finder's guide because it at least eliminates a researcher's having to listen to an entire tape for usable information.

Figure 8, page 23, shows two sample INTERVIEW CONTENTS sheets. By using these finder's aids, a person researching the effects of the Depression on various segments of the population would quickly be able to locate one such discussion on the McMann tape.

Even if one is planning to index transcripts, the indexing of tape contents is still an important procedure. There will be patrons who prefer to listen to the tape for further information, as well as those who may wish to clarify or amplify their reading of a portion of the transcript. In such cases, the INTERVIEW CONTENTS sheet will prove valuable.

Indexing Transcripts

A table of contents, an abbreviated form of transcript index, may be a sufficient help to researchers if one has a small collection and short interviews.

It may be quite general in nature, simply pointing out what is unique about a memoir and the main subjects discussed in its dialogue. A quick glance at this introductory page can give the researcher some idea of the document's value for him/her and on what pages to look for information. Although a table of contents is most often prepared from final typed copy, it might prove useful to compile one as soon as a rough transcript is available.

A table of contents may follow any format which seems most helpful and clear for users. It may be a separate page, as in figure 25, or merely an expanded preface page, wherein is usually found a brief biographical sketch and summary of the interview's contents.

An index at the end of each final typed manuscript might also be considered if a program plans a sizable collection or lengthy memoirs. Available time and personnel will be factors in deciding whether to compose simple alphabetical indexes of proper names mentioned in the interviews or comprehensive proper name and subject indexes. There is controversy over the merits of each. Programs which favor only an *indexing of proper names* believe that researchers realize they must read an entire interview to get the flavor of the historical source and the context of its information. Programs which undertake *indexing on both a proper name and subject basis* feel that despite the amount of extra work involved, such a comprehensive system saves the researcher's time and energy, especially with long memoirs.

Planning for a transcript indexing system is essential. One must begin to

DR. EDWIN A. LEE MEMOIR

TABLE OF CONTENTS

Family background 1

Education 4
    boarding school, Tougaloo High School

Talladega College 21

Morehouse College 25

Meharry Medical School 35

Marriage, 1941 47

Army experiences (93rd Division) 49
    Pennsylvania, Arizona, California
    South Pacific, Phillipine Islands

Residency in St. Louis 80

Establishing medical practice in Springfield 91

Prejudice, discrimination in Springfield 93

Church membership 98

Civic activities 100

Springfield School Board 106

Copley First Citizen of the Year Award 111

Fig. 25. A table of contents—an abbreviated transcript index.

think of transcripts as parts of a collection rather than as individual memoirs. Each will of course be specifically indexed by names, events, and geographical locations. But there will be a need for general terms to describe less specific subjects discussed in the interviews, for example, Mines and Mining. Although individually prepared, transcript indexes should be compiled so that there is maximum standardization in the forms of proper names, and consistency in the terminology used to designate the same subjects in all indexes.

The purpose of each part of a system, the indexes of transcripts and the card catalog of the whole collection, is the same—to aid in retrieval of information. But the scope of the terms used to describe the transcript will obviously be narrower than that of the same terms used to describe the contents of the collection as a whole. For instance, the names of coal mines mentioned during discussion of a narrator's years in coal mining would appear in a transcript index, as would the term Mines and Mining, Coal. The transcript would be included in the card catalog under the heading Mines and Mining, Coal. If there were only general discussion of coal mining in a transcript, the term Mines and Mining, Coal, would appear in the index and the transcript would also be referenced under Mines and Mining, Coal in the card catalog.

An independent oral history center will have relatively little trouble establishing continuity in its information retrieval system. But if a program is affiliated with a library there are some limitations and problems in adding interview transcripts to the library catalog. Transcript indexing terms can to a certain extent be made uniform with the library's policies for its subject entries, but in most cases one will have to employ more general subject headings. Since the subject headings selected for indexing transcripts will have to be consistent with those in use for the library, it is desirable and probably necessary that oral history catalog cards be filed separately.

If one is set up independently and is free to decide upon a system of indexing terminology and subject catalog headings, he/she will want a system that is most workable for his/her program. There is no standard set of subject headings used in common by all libraries, so it would be wise to examine the following reference books to become familiar with the various descriptive systems.

Library of Congress Subject Headings, edited by Marguerite Quattlebaum

Sears List of Subject Headings, 10th ed., ed. by Barbara M. Westby (New York: Wilson, 1972)

Cross-Reference Index, A Subject Heading Guide, ed. by Thomas V. Atkins (New York: Bowker, 1974). The *Cross-Reference Index* is a useful guide for comparing various systems and beginning to feel which kinds of terms relate best to one's subject matter. It lists subject headings from six sources:

1. *Library of Congress Subject Headings*, which is used in catalogs of most universities and research libraries
2. *Sears List of Subject Headings*, which is used mainly in catalogs of school and public libraries

3. *The Readers' Guide to Periodical Literature*, an index listing of popular, nontechnical, and a few scholarly magazines in many fields
4. *The New York Times Index*, useful for current events and up-to-date statistical information
5. *Public Affairs Information Service Bulletin*, an index of current books, pamphlets, periodicals, and other material dealing with economics and public affairs
6. *Business Periodicals Index*, a list of articles from selected periodicals dealing with economics, labor, management, and taxation, among other subjects.

If part of a collection is a series of interviews on art or legal history, for instance, one may also want to consult a specialized art or legal index to find the terminology most familiar to researchers in that field.

A person may want to follow only one of these heading systems, but more likely will find some combination to be more appropriate and workable for the oral history format. What is important is that the words chosen to designate a subject should be usable, up-to-date, and pertinent to the particular subject matter.

Indexing an oral history transcript is not a simple task. Transcripts cover many different subjects, and even those which discuss the same subject often do so from different angles, to different extents, and with varying degrees of emphasis. Given such a wide range, it would seem a difficult task to develop a system of descriptors which would bring continuity to an entire collection. It is probably only through the perspective to be gained by one person working with all of the transcripts that the necessarily relative judgments can be made and a cohesive indexing system implemented. Though there are some general guidelines, expertise will come mainly through practice. For an idea of the methods used, *Indexes and Indexing* by Robert Collison (New York: De Graff, 1972) may be helpful reading.

When beginning to index, one must first read an entire transcript for perspective. The INTERVIEW CONTENTS sheet will prove helpful, although it can not be relied upon to supply a thorough picture of an interview. Having read through an interview, one should sit down with a box file of blank three-by-five-inch cards, which can later be filed alphabetically, and begin to carefully reread the transcript.

Make note, as in the sample three-by-five cards in figure 26, of all *significantly discussed* proper names in a transcript. Since much oral history information is local in nature, one must carefully include all significant proper names, not just those which are well known. Enter one name per card and indicate at least the narrator's initials somewhere on each card. Such a precaution is important when working with several transcripts at the same time for it is necessary to be certain that the forms of various names agree.

Beginning with general subject headings is easiest, when planning to index subjects as well as proper names presented in an interview. It is wise to use a

Dr. Edwin A. Lee   58

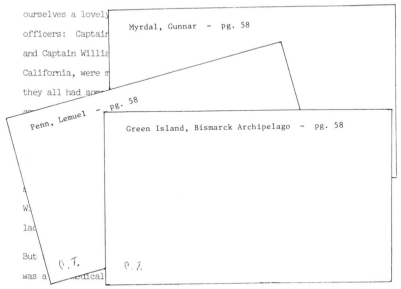

and that is Captian Lemuel Penn. To those who do not recognize this
name, Captain Penn is the Army officer who was shot down in Georgia
during the late 1950's as he was going back to his home in Washington
after having attended a summer camp. He was shot as he drove along
the highway, by some white people who apparently did it for no reason
other than the fact that they hated black people. It was very sad
when I learned of this, and the country felt very bad about it. He was
a sociologist and was a principal of a high school in Washington, D. C.
In fact, if you will read Gunnar Myrdal's American Dilemma, you will
find Captain Penn's name in the front as one of the contributors to
this book.

As I was sitting in my hut one day on Green Island, I got a telephone

Fig. 26. Sample proper names for an index.

separate card to note each heading and its page references, as shown in figure 27. Jot down enough about each discussion of a subject to be able to distinguish it from others. This is a time-consuming process, but will save a second intensive reading by adequately identifying various subjects from the very beginning. If one aspect of a subject, for example, discrimination in education, warrants its own subject heading, some revision may be necessary.

Making these general descriptors as appropriate and concise as possible is the next task. Overly generalized entries, which have long lists of page references, should be made more specific. Specific entries will be more accurate and provide quick reference. In figure 28, the middle card obviously gives a more valuable picture of the different aspects of education discussed in one transcript. The bottom card shows the addition of a main subject heading.

One must be careful not to become a prisoner of the chosen subject headings. If an oral history program is interviewing various educators, for instance, the system of concise headings on the middle card in figure 28 makes sense. However, if the series of interviews had been conducted with various members of the black community, it is likely that the issue of discrimination would be sufficiently important to be a main subject heading. In that case, the index

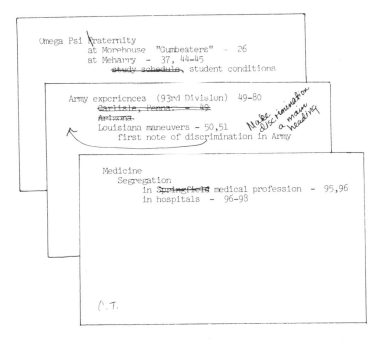

Fig. 27. The beginning steps in compiling a subject heading index.

cards would have to be revised to reflect more accurately the discussions in the transcript, as on the bottom card in figure 28.

Subdivisions of an extensive subject should be made from a consistent point of view: for instance, geographically, chronologically, or by more specific topics. For example, if a narrator discusses his early education in a Mexican village and his subsequent language problems while continuing school in Texas, those topics should be noted, as on the top card in figure 29. But in the order shown, the topics would not be particularly helpful to someone using the index. A better arrangement is shown on the bottom card in figure 29. The main heading, EDUCATION, is divided geographically as well as chronologically, thus providing a more accurate reflection of the interview contents. While not vitally important to the preparation of preliminary subject cards, such organizing principles should be kept in mind so that final indexing can be done with the least amount of revision and rereading.

Maintaining a discriminating eye is, therefore, the key concept in indexing a transcript. A long index may look impressive but be totally useless. Researchers will be looking for fresh information—some material of substance about a particular subject, person, place or event. So it is not necessary or even desirable to compile references for every occurrence of a name or subject, as in figure 30. References to Norman Thomas and Eugene Debs would only take up a researcher's time, not give anything of informational value in return.

Cross-references may be needed. When it has been decided which proper names and subject headings to include in a transcript's index, review them with thought to any necessary cross-references, particularly SEE and SEE ALSO references. For an index of the depth needed for most oral history transcripts, few such cross-references will have to be included. It is mainly in cases where a choice between two nearly synonymous terms needs to be made, as in AGRICULTURE and FARMS AND FARMING, that an indexer must be concerned with cross-referencing. One needs to consider the scope of each memoir and make decisions based on the way certain terms relate to a transcript's subject matter in order to ensure concise indexing.

Cross-references must also be worked out with an eye to precedent. The terminology used in one memoir index must also be acceptable to and coordinate with that used in other indexes and in any future cataloging done in an entire collection. For instance, even though AGRICULTURE might not seem to be too general for the subject matter of one transcript, it might be best to use FARMS AND FARMING as a main heading if it is anticipated that further interviews will be conducted which will primarily discuss other aspects of agriculture, such as maintaining lemon groves or orchards, or other specific farming methods. The transcript index would thus contain the following entries:

Agriculture. SEE Farms and Farming
Farms and Farming, pp. 6–17

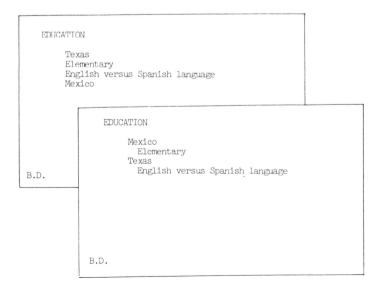

EDUCATION - - 24-27, 32, 40-44, 49-52

EDUCATION,

    Religious 24-27
    Religious - curriculum 32, 36
    Medical 40-44
    Discrimination 49-52

C.T.

DISCRIMINATION,

    Educational 49-52
    Housing
    Legal

C.T.

Fig. 28. Appropriate and concise subject descriptors for the final index of a transcript.

EDUCATION

    Texas
    Elementary
    English versus Spanish language
    Mexico

EDUCATION

    Mexico
      Elementary
    Texas
      English versus Spanish language

B.D.

B.D.

Fig. 29. Sample index cards for extensive subjects.

The manner in which place, institution, and government agency names will be indexed should also be decided at this point. Note, for instance, that in the index to the Dale Charles Memoir, figure 31, Dixon State School, Department of Mental Health, and Jacksonville State Hospital do not reflect the fact that they are associated with Illinois. Because of the local nature of much oral history material, many programs refer to the locations only of places, institutions, and agencies which are outside the state or region: in this example, Atlanta, Georgia.

However, if the scope of a collection of memoirs is such that it encompasses discussions of widespread places and events, specific locations may have to be noted consistently and a certain amount of repetition tolerated to minimize confusion for users.

```
Q:  What can you tell us is your opinion and your personal view
    of Norman Thomas?

A:  I thought he was a pretty nice man.  I voted for him all the
    time.  I voted for Debs and I think he was the first one I
    voted for.  Oh yes, see, my dad used to get the Appeal to
    Reason when I was a kid.  I was exposed to the socialist paper
    as a young lad.  A lot of things that I read there made a lot
    of good sense to me and I could see that there was a lot to it.
```

Fig. 30. Incidental references which should not be indexed.

```
                        INDEX

                DALE CHARLES MEMOIR

    Atlanta, Georgia    8
    Bettag, Otto    1
    Dixon State School    3
    Elgin State Hospital    1, 6, 7
    Food Manager, duties of    4, 10
    Illinois Security Hospital    1
    Jacksonville State Hospital    4, 11, 12
    Master Menu Plan    3
    Mental Health, Department of    1
    Mentally retarded    3, 4, 5
    Patients, as employees    5, 6
            decrease in number of    11, 12
            and their relations with staff    7, 13, 14
    Public Safety, Department of SEE Mental Health, Department of
    Socialization    13
    State Hospital farms    8
    Uniforms, staff    9, 10
```

Fig. 31. Sample format for a final transcript index.

An Authority File

Once the main subject headings to be used in an index have been decided, they essentially become permanent. They should be used in any other transcripts indexed and, when appropriate, in the preparation of a card catalog of an entire collection. One means of ensuring continuity in terminology from one index to another and to an eventual card catalog is to compile a Subject Heading Control List, often called an Authority File. This is an alphabetical listing of all subject headings, their subdivisions and cross-references, and the forms of all proper names one has decided to use. If a subject card catalog is to be established, it could serve as the Authority File. But if the catalog is large or is located away from the staff's work area, the less cumbersome Authority File is more convenient.

An Authority File is part of an internal tracing system to be used by the oral history staff. It is particularly important if one needs to rely upon short-term workers or volunteer help to do indexing or cataloging rather than on one person who carries the whole system in his/her head. The Authority File is different and separate from an actual card catalog in that no specific memoirs are detailed. It simply makes possible, when undertaking further indexing or cataloging projects, a quick review of the headings used in completed indexes or the subject card catalog in order to prevent the addition of terms which may be contradictory or superfluous. If one has a very small collection or wants to limit the depth of indexing to only the main subjects of oral history transcripts, a typed *list* of official headings may be sufficient. Otherwise, a file of the cards used to prepare the index is most practical: it can be easily expanded and adjusted (see figure 32).

Cataloging a Collection

By the time one has indexed several transcripts, he/she is undoubtedly familiar enough with the process of defining subject matter to establish a "narrator catalog" of oral history transcripts. The purpose of this catalog is to give users a general idea of the contents of each transcript. Arranged alphabetically by narrators' surnames, this catalog will be helpful to researchers wanting to know about specific persons' memoirs. For programs with minimum financing, this can also serve in place of a subject card catalog, although using only a narrator catalog will require more research time. The catalog may take one of two forms: a sheaf or notebook catalog, or a card catalog.

A sheaf or notebook catalog may be adequate to serve the user of programs with limited resources or small collections. For this type of catalog, a page for each interview is prepared and inserted in a loose-leaf binder. Each page should include enough information to steer a researcher in the proper direction: at least the narrator's name and the focus of his/her interview, the length of the interview in pages and hours, and the interview's status (whether usage is restricted). This data can be pulled from a transcript's preface page, the

INTERVIEW CONTENTS sheet, and the processing section of the INTERVIEW DATA SHEET. However, if one is continuing to add memoirs to the collection, this notebook format is not the most desirable. The added expense of purchasing files for a narrator card catalog will prove worthwhile, for one can then more easily keep pace with an expanding collection.

A *narrator* card catalog set up in a unit card format, similar to the examples in figure 33, is strongly recommended. Its flexibility makes it a superior alternative to pages in a notebook. A catalog in this three-by-five-inch format would arrange interviews alphabetically by narrators' surnames. Sufficient information should be put on these cards to provide users with a specific idea of which tapes or transcripts will be of value to them. Therefore, the more information included, the better; more than one card may be used if needed.

An explanation of the necessary data to be recorded follows. Refer to figure 33 for placement on the cards.

1. Narrator's name in inverted form, surname first; narrator's birthdate; date of death, when applicable.

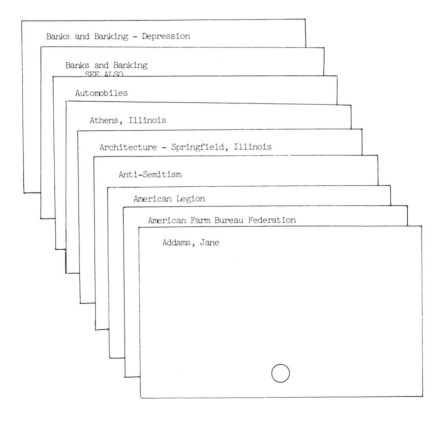

Fig. 32. Sample Authority File.

2. A breakdown of the major topics discussed during the interviews. Because each memoir has been indexed and subject headings have been established for describing the interview's contents, one should be familiar enough with the contents of the transcript to easily compose a brief synopsis of it. To conserve space, this should be written in a telegraphic style, eliminating all but the highlights of the discussion. It should begin with an identifying phrase about the narrator, perhaps his/her lifelong occupation or connection with the main subject discussed, that is, why he/she was interviewed. Following this,

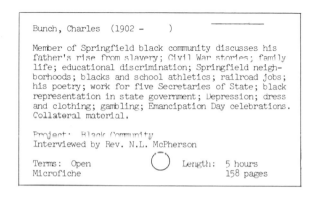

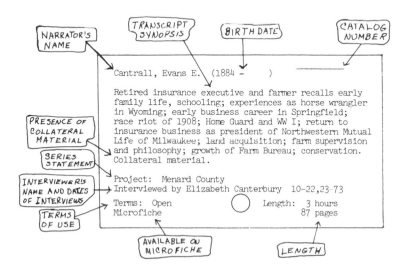

Fig. 33. Sample formats for a narrator card catalog.
Compare lower card with notes in figure 36.

each major topic discussed should be noted. Brevity is all-important. What is desired here is a short biographical sketch—experiences of the narrator and events to which he/she was witness that make the interview valuable historical material. Topics can be rearranged from their order within the interview, especially chronologically, to make a more coherent thumbnail sketch. The presence of collateral material such as photographs or journals should be indicated on the card. As these are often filed separately from tapes or transcripts, a researcher will probably remain ignorant of their existence without such a notation.

3. A series statement, that is, whether the interview was done in connection with others on a particular theme or subject such as coal mining, farming, or Prohibition. This will let the researcher know that there are other related tapes or transcripts in the collection. Some programs also note whether such a project is complete or still active, whether other interviews are still planned or in process.

4. The interviewer's name and the date on which the interview was conducted. If the memoir contains more than one interview, include all dates.

5. Terms of use, that is, whether the interview is open, restricted, or closed. *Open* means that the narrator has fully released his/her rights to the interview material and researchers may freely read, cite, and quote it. *Restricted* means that the material has some restrictions on usage, that the narrator prefers not to be quoted, or that he/she wants certain portions to remain confidential. *Closed* interviews are in most cases not available at all to researchers for a stated period of time, often until the death of the narrator. In the case of restricted and closed interviews, the notations to that effect on these catalog cards should be detailed and amplified on the INTERVIEW DATA SHEET and within the transcript's preface as well as on the legal release. If an interview has been transcribed, but is not yet in final form, such amplifications should be noted on a sheet of paper attached to the front of the transcript. Such a precaution will ensure that users, who probably will not see the actual legal release, are informed of restrictions on use.

6. The length of the interview, both in hours and number of typed pages. It is best to pencil in the number of pages until a final copy has been typed.

7. A notation of whether the interview is available on microfiche (as discussed in Step 8).

8. Accession numbers, in the top right-hand corner or at the left margin. Various shelving systems will be discussed at a later point.

Many programs with adequate personnel and financing also catalog their interviews by subject in a *subject* card catalog. Researchers investigating a specific subject rather than an individual will find it more direct to begin in this section of the card catalog rather than in the narrator catalog, particularly in oral history collections that contain many interviews.

Again, if a collection is to be housed in a library which insists upon the use of its cataloging system, be sure to follow their guidelines. However, if one is free to develop an independent information retrieval system, here are some points which should be considered.

Small collections may want to compile a *dictionary* card catalog, as in figure 34, in which main entry (narrator or unit cards) and subject cards are interfiled in one alphabet. This arrangement, traditionally used in American libraries, is familiar to patrons. Its principal drawback is that as its size increases, so does the time needed by a user to thoroughly investigate the collection's holdings on a particular subject.

Card catalogs in which author, title, and subject are separately arranged are also common, especially in larger libraries. Such an arrangement makes it easier to search for a subject and its subdivisions since there are no interruptions by unrelated cards. Oral history material, however, is most efficiently categorized in only two, rather than the above-mentioned three, ways: author

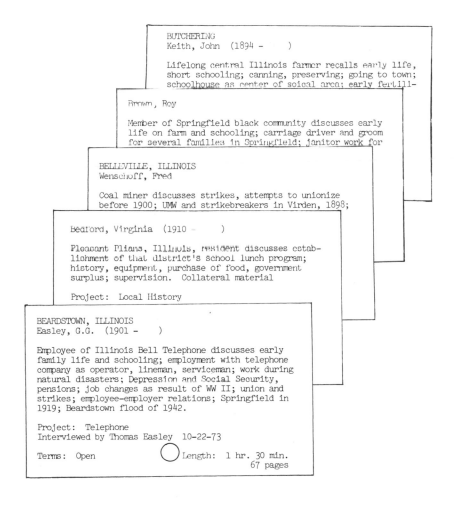

Fig. 34. Sample dictionary catalog cards.

(narrator) and subject. The subject card catalog should be complete enough to analyze holdings thoroughly and yet not be so complicated or overly detailed that a researcher is apt to waste time or get lost.

It should be determined at this point whether the cataloging system will include sufficient information for easy, unassisted use or whether a staff person will have to be available to interpret data and answer questions. A self-help catalog should live up to its name or have a set of instructions nearby. If the terms of some legal releases stipulate that certain material be restricted or closed, a staff person will most likely be necessary. Estimate who the users will be and tailor the card catalog to be most workable for them.

Even if you have not previously indexed the transcripts, subject cataloging can be done, employing a method similar to that used to index transcripts, but without concern for page references. Much of the information needed to catalog a transcript by subject can be gleaned from the synopsis of the interview on the unit card in the narrator card catalog. But there is no guarantee that a unit card summary, as in figure 33, contains all topics which should be included in a subject card catalog. Remember, these synopses are meant to reflect the *major* subjects and names. A unit card does not provide much room, and some important subjects or names mentioned in the transcript may have been necessarily left out.

The transcripts themselves should be read for perspective and notes made about the various topics of discussion, as shown in figure 35. The cataloger should work with these notes and choose the offiicial terminology to be used. The number of pages devoted to various topics is also a helpful indication of which subjects are important enough to be official headings. A cataloger may decide that the Charles Bunch transcript should be mentioned under the following headings in a subject catalog: (1) RAILROADS, (2) BLACKS AND POLITICS, (3) BLACKS AND DISCRIMINATION, (4) DEPRESSION, (5) EMANCIPATION DAY, and (6) CLOTHING AND DRESS (see figure 35). An Authority File of these terms, as discussed earlier, should then be started.

If indexes for individual transcripts have already been compiled, the task of putting together a subject card catalog will not be difficult. This catalog will not be simply the sum of the transcript indexes, because the catalog headings will pertain wherever possible to the entire transcript or otherwise to its major portions. However, because of the often geographically limited nature of many oral history collections and because the subjects discussed are often locally specific, one should attempt to be as specific in the choice of subject card catalog headings as users will find necessary.

The descriptors used in the indexes should be employed when possible; the subject headings should be coordinated with the transcript index headings through the Authority File. From the subject card catalog, then, a user can quickly identify which transcripts discuss the subjects being researched, go to a transcript's index, and find the specific pages needed. If descriptors used in

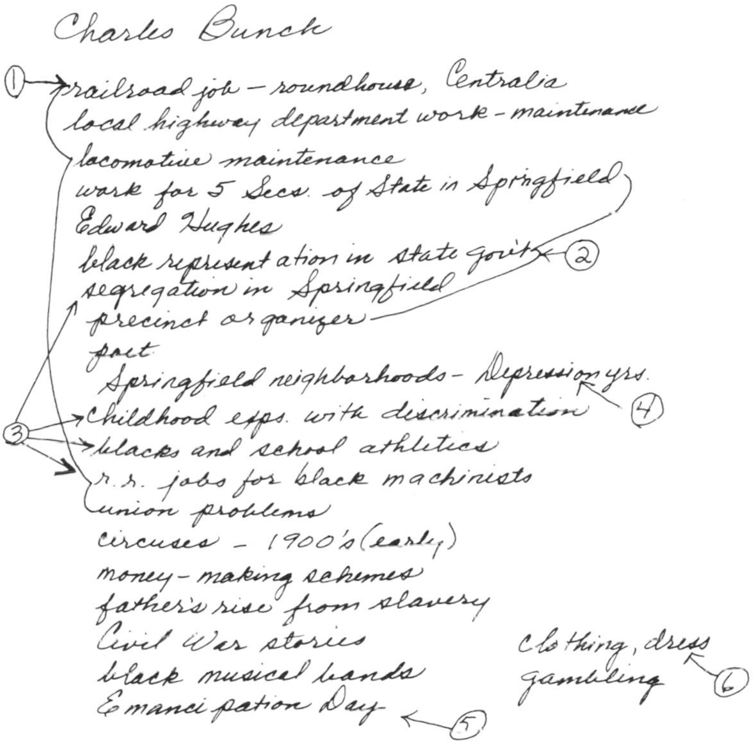

Charles Bunch

(1) railroad job – roundhouse, Centralia
local highway department work – maintenance
locomotive maintenance
work for 5 Secs. of State in Springfield
Edward Hughes
black representation in state gov't (2)
segregation in Springfield
precinct organizer
poet
Springfield neighborhoods – Depression yrs. (4)
(3) Childhood exps. with discrimination
blacks and school athletics
r.r. jobs for black machinists
union problems
circuses – 1900's (early)
money-making schemes
father's rise from slavery
Civil War stories
black musical bands
Emancipation Day (5)
Clothing, dress
gambling (6)

Fig. 35. Cataloging notes made from a reading of a transcript.

the indexes and card catalog differ, the user will always wonder whether he/she has located all the material being sought.

Indexing the oral history collection for a subject card catalog may be done in three ways. First, the unit card system can be used as the basis for multiple entries for an oral history transcript. Make as many duplicates of the basic unit card as needed to have one copy for each subject heading which is applicable to a particular memoir. Then type one of these subject headings above the main entry—the narrator's name—at the top of each of these duplicate cards. The result is a subject catalog card.

In the lower right corner of figure 36 is the unit card for the John Keith Memoir. Above it is the series of cards made from it for use in a subject card catalog. Each subject underlined on the original unit card has become an official subject heading and has been overtyped on a duplicate card.

A variation of this unit card system entails the same duplication procedure, but has the appropriate subject headings typed only on oversized guide cards. For instance, in figure 37, the subject heading BANKS AND BANKING is typed on a guide card. Immediately following it in the file would be, alpha-

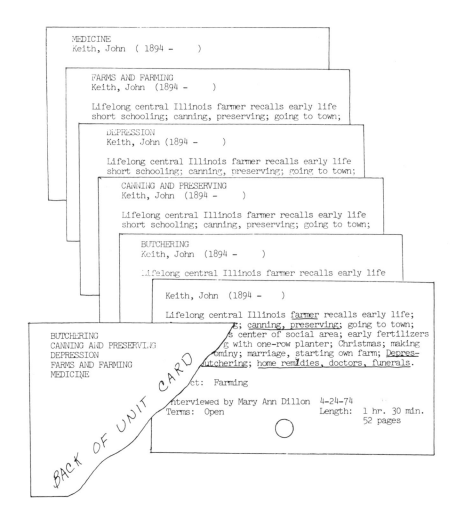

Fig. 36. A variation of the unit card system of indexing.

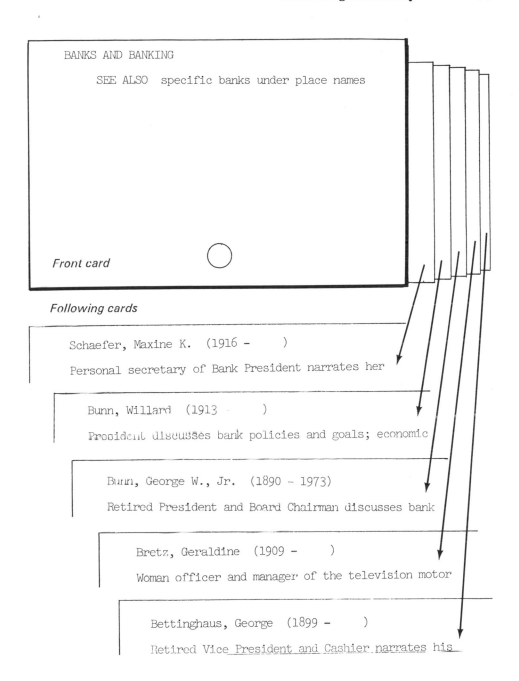

BANKS AND BANKING

    SEE ALSO specific banks under place names

Front card

Following cards

Schaefer, Maxine K. (1916 -   )

Personal secretary of Bank President narrates her

Bunn, Willard (1913 -   )

President discusses bank policies and goals; economic

Bunn, George W., Jr. (1890 - 1973)

Retired President and Board Chairman discusses bank

Bretz, Geraldine (1909 -   )

Woman officer and manager of the television motor

Bettinghaus, George (1899 -   )

Retired Vice President and Cashier narrates his

Fig. 37. Another form of the unit card subject catalog, utilizing
oversized guide cards.

betically arranged, duplicate unit cards of all the memoirs which discuss that subject. In this setup, the subject headings are more obvious and easy to find because of the divisions created by the oversized guide cards. In addition, it is recommended that these headings be typed in capital letters.

Third, if duplication is too expensive, the subject guide card concept can still prove workable. Only the names of the narrators whose interviews discuss a subject need be listed, alphabetically, either directly on the guide card or on separate cards following the guide card, as shown in figure 38. Such a subject card catalog would have to be used in close conjunction with the basic narrator catalog and would entail a longer procedure for users, who must flip back and forth between the two files to find what they need. Adding new names to existing lists would also prove time-consuming.

For any of these three methods, it is important that the original unit card carries, on its back, a record of all subject headings made for that memoir. This makes it easier to retrace the cataloging steps whenever necessary—whether to recatalog, change subject headings, or add new headings to an entry (see figure 36). Concise and accurate subject headings are important.

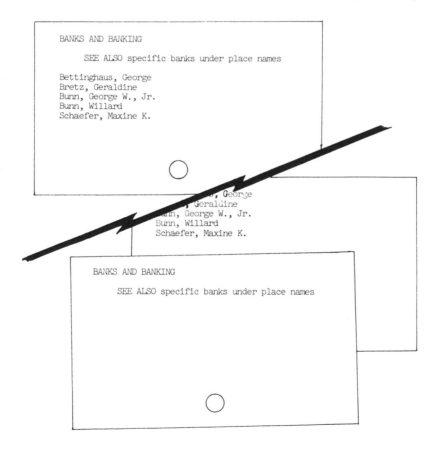

Fig. 38. Less expensive variations of the subject guide card system.

Refer to the discussion on the indexing of transcripts for other tips on compiling the information necessary for subject cataloging.

Initiating a workable set of cross-references is another aspect of preparing the catalog. The use of SEE and SEE ALSO eliminates duplication of terms and should lead the user along a path of subject headings and related entries directly to the unit cards of the transcripts which will be of value. It is important to keep in mind who the users will be and what key words they would be likely to think of when looking for certain information. This may be the main consideration when there is a choice among several synonyms or closely related words.

A SEE reference tells a user to look under an equivalent main term because the subject heading he/she has chosen is not used in the catalog (see figure 39). Well-known abbreviations should be cross-referenced with cards containing the full titles, for example, a card for IWW would contain a SEE reference to INDUSTRIAL WORKERS OF THE WORLD.

A SEE ALSO reference gives subject headings for corresponding, comparable, and related material in the card catalog. Such references are put in alphabetical order, if more than one, and point to more specific aspects of the main term, as in figure 40. The SEE ALSO reference is also a general information reference. It refers the user from a general subject to the specific instances of which it is composed, as in figure 38.

An Internal Tracing System

As memoirs are added to a collection, there will be an expansion and probable shift of the descriptors used. To ease this process of change and the retrieval of cards that are no longer useful or that need to be expanded upon, an internal tracing system should be implemented. Two aspects of such a system

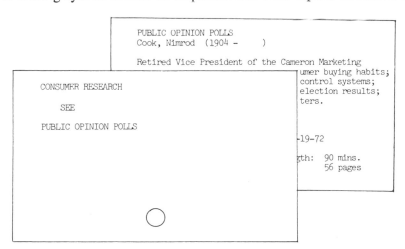

Fig. 39. A SEE reference.

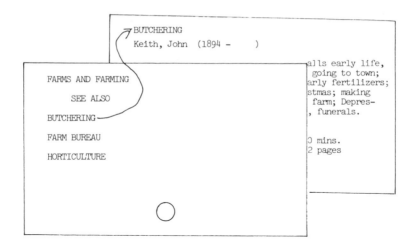

Fig. 40. A SEE ALSO reference.

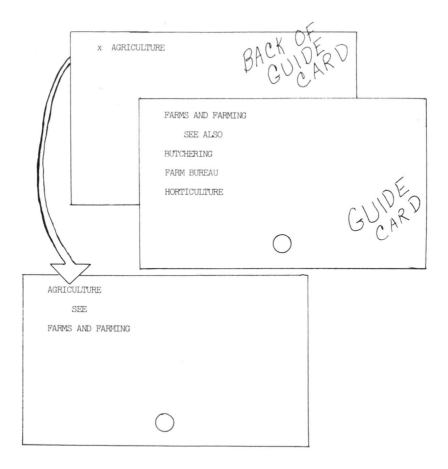

Fig. 41. Sample cross-reference notation "x".

have already been discussed. These are (1) the Authority File, which is a compilation of the subjects and proper names used in indexing and cataloging transcripts, primarily for internal office use; and (2) a record of all subject entries made for a memoir, carried on the back of each unit card in the narrator card catalog. The latter facilitates retracing cataloging steps should it be necessary to make additions or changes to previously cataloged transcripts.

The third part of a tracing system is really an abridgement of the Authority File on each subject guide card. Cross-reference notations are made on the backs of the guide cards in the subject card catalog. They coordinate official subject headings with the cross-references made from them. The tracing system makes possible the easy retrieval of an entire series of related cards if changes are necessary. Two such cross-reference notations are "x" and "xx".

A notation of x on the back of an official subject guide card (one with unit cards behind it) means, "Under the following term in the card catalog there is a SEE reference to this official heading." The middle card of figure 41 is a guide card with the official heading FARMS AND FARMING. The x-referenced term (but not official subject heading) AGRICULTURE is noted on its back. The x alerts staff members to the guide card with the term AGRICULTURE and its SEE reference to the official heading, FARMS AND FARMING, shown in the upper part of figure 41.

A notation of xx on the back of an official guide card says, "Under the following official subject heading in the card catalog there is a SEE ALSO reference to this official heading." As shown in the lower part of figure 42, a guide card with BUTCHERING as its official heading would have noted on its back, xx FARMS AND FARMING. The xx would alert a staff member to the guide card shown in the upper part of figure 42 with FARMS and FARMING and its SEE ALSO references, including BUTCHERING.

A Shelf List

Many oral history centers shelve their transcripts alphabetically by narrators' surnames. Their narrator catalog then takes on the added function of a shelf list for the collection. The one disadvantage of this approach is that it scatters memoirs focusing on a single subject.

Some programs conduct interviews around such specific projects or themes as coal mining or World War II, and therefore prefer to code their transcripts numerically. Six digits will adequately cover additions to a growing collection, and certain blocks of numbers can be set aside for projects still in process. This can be done starting with 000001, 000002, and so on, or in any other manner that facilitates retrieval. Such a process is not dissimilar to the traditional library practice of subject classification. Some programs may prefer to number their interviews according to the order in which they were conducted and received in the oral history office. This is often referred to as an accession numbering system.

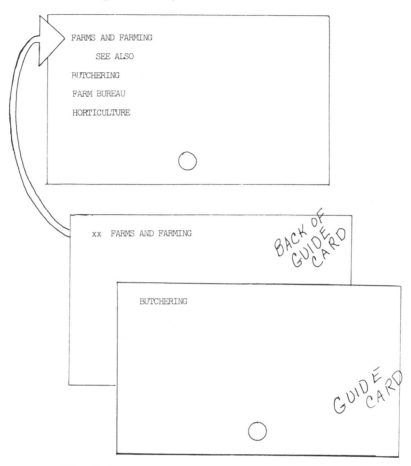

Fig. 42. Sample cross-reference notation "xx".

Whichever system is chosen, the number allotted each memoir should be noted both on its unit card and on the bound memoir itself. A separate shelf list file should also be compiled in this case, which would list the memoirs by number as they are shelved. In addition, collateral materials might be indicated on the unit cards by the use of subscripts and either shelved directly with their respective transcripts or separately according to the same numbering system. A collection arranged purely according to accession numbers would have guide cards perhaps only every one hundred cards, and solely for easy retrieval of the particular memoir or a certain number.

For further reading about cataloging, the following books provide good and very basic coverage of the subject: *Library Cataloging: A Guide for a Basic Course* by John Immroth and Jay Daily (Metuchen, N.J.: Scarecrow, 1971) and *Introduction to Cataloging*, volumes 1 and 2 by John J. Boll (New York: McGraw-Hill, 1970, 1974).

In California, individual cataloging systems have been integrated to form one comprehensive card catalog of oral history collections throughout the state. The California State Library has initiated the California Bibliographic

Center for Oral History, and asks that libraries, historical societies, and museums send them a unit catalog card describing each interview they have. Such use of a central filing system for an entire region or state is convenient for users and, at the same time, is a tremendous boon to individual oral history programs in their task of dissemination.

Step 8: Reaching the Public

Some offices have no adequate physical space for users, being primarily collecting and processing centers. If an office has this problem, it is particularly important to inform the public about the availability of its collection and to use every means possible to make the collection accessible through other facilities such as historical or university libraries.

The methods used to reach the public will vary with one's resources, the nature and scope of a collection, and the groups or institutions in an area with which cooperative arrangements can be made. This section of the manual will discuss some of the more common approaches to the task of disseminating oral history memoirs.

Book Catalogs

Many oral history programs regularly publish either a printed book catalog of their holdings or at least a typed list of their annual accessions. These serve partially as finder's aids, but they also publicize the nature and growth of oral history collections. They are advantageous in that, unlike a card catalog, any number of copies can be made available, and the collection can be consulted outside the oral history office.

Columbia University, which houses the oldest and largest oral history collection in the country, publishes a model catalog. It is by far the most extensive and elaborate of such books. The entire collection is organized into a single alphabetical sequence and indexed by subjects, projects, and proper names.

The format best suited to one's oral history collection will depend on the purpose of the catalog, the quantity of information included, the financial resources and methods of printing available, and the needs of the users. The simplest form of citation to follow is the same used for the card catalog. Many oral history programs simply duplicate their shelf list cards in alphabetical order onto an 8½-by-11-inch page format. This at least gives the information necessary for researchers to make further inquiries about specific interviews.

Figure 43 shows one possibility, a shelf list in book format. This initial catalog could be expanded as one is able, by arranging interviews topically or according to projects as well as biographically. A further aid would be the addition of a complete index to the interview entries, the only place where topical distinctions should be made. Some programs may prefer to include an in-process section at the end which lists those oral history tapes received but not yet in finished form.

Davenport, Don; Evans, Barb; Ginder, George;
    McCoach, Caroline

Former one-room school teachers and three former
one-room school students compare one-room school
to two-room school; student attitudes in one-
room school.

Project: One-Room Schools

Interviewed by Jane Stout   2-16-72

Terms: Open   Length: 30 mins.
                                 13 pages

Davison, Edward (1908 -   )

Retired Vice President and Controller discusses
Accrual and Proof Departments; Ridgely-Farmers
State Bank closure; change in banking practices.

Project: Springfield Marine Bank

Interviewed by John Bucari   7-31-73

Terms: Open   Length: 1 hour
                                 30 pages

Day, Phoebe Mitchell (1895 -   )

Native of Springfield black community discusses
early family life and schooling; work as beau-
tician; husband's furniture refinishing business; work as matron in state offices; race
riot of 1908.

Project: Black Community

Interviewed by Rev. N.L. McPherson 3-25-74

Terms: Open   Length: 90 mins.
                                 39 pages

DeLong, Eleanor (1911 -   )

Hospital laundry technician at Jacksonville State
Hospital, Jacksonville, Illinois, discusses early
life and employment history; laundry operations;
use of patient labor; hiring practices; effects
of Depression; 1929 fire; new laundry building.

Project: Mental Health Care

Interviewed by Rodger Streitmatter 10-11-72

Terms: Open   Length: 45 mins.
                                 33 pages

Dunham, James (1934 -   )

Former city commissioner, Springfield, Illinois,
narrates his reaction to John F. Kennedy's
assassination; churches filled; validity of
Warren Commission Report.

Project: John F. Kennedy Assassination

Interviewed by Robert Dixon 2-24-72

Terms: Open   Length: 15 mins.
                                       pages

Dunigan, Agnes (1900 -   )

Springfield, Illinois, resident recounts life
during World War II; draft board; rationing;
home front; civil defense.

Project: Homefront in World War II

Interviewed by JoAnne Wheeler 10-25-72

Terms: Open   Length: 45 mins.
                                       pages

Easley, G. G. (1901 -   )

Employee of Illinois Bell Telephone discusses
early family life and schooling; employment with
telephone company as operator, lineman, service-
man; work during natural disasters; Depression
and Social Security, pensions; job changes as
result of WW II; union and strikes; employee-
employer relations; Springfield in 1919;
Beardstown flood of 1942.

Project: Telephone
Interviewed by Thomas Easley 10-22-73

Terms: Open   Length: 1 hr. 30 mins..
                                 67 pages

Ebers, Herschel W. (1906 -   )

Retired Vice President and Cashier discusses the
Depression and bank run; changes in banking practices; relations of employee to customer; rationing during World War II.

Project: Springfield Marine Bank

Interviewed by John Bucari 8-22-73

Terms: Open   Length: 1 hour
                                 30 pages

Fig. 43. A shelf list in book format.

The final choice will depend on financial resources and one's assessment of the value of a printed catalog for prospective users. The only word of caution offered is that deciding to undertake a project such as this will involve a commitment to also undertake the publication of supplementary or revised editions as the collection grows. The cost of keeping a book catalog current is high. For this reason, many programs prefer to print short yearly accession lists.

The *National Union Catalog of Manuscript Collections* is an alphabetical listing of the latest manuscripts (and oral history transcripts) cataloged by the Library of Congress and other North American libraries. Generally to be found in all larger libraries, this book catalog is an ideal means of wide dissemination of an oral history collection. The Library of Congress will supply Data Sheets on which to enter information about the memoirs in one's collection. In this way, the Library of Congress is able to translate information from many different types of oral history repositories into uniform entries for inclusion in their volume. The Data Sheet explains the name of a collection (at least ten memoirs related to a certain subject); its location; the approximate years it covers; its size; the narrators involved; and a description of the contents, including important persons, places, and events involved.

The information on these Data Sheets is printed on three-by-five-inch cards, compiled, and published serially in book form to be distributed to larger libraries throughout the country. For further information and for Data Sheets, write to:

Editor, NUCMC
Descriptive Cataloging Division
Manuscripts Division
Library of Congress
Washington, DC 20540

Regional and Statewide Cooperation

Some scattered regional and statewide projects have developed along similar lines. Many of them have tried to compile bibliographies of the oral history collections in their region to build awareness among interested individuals and institutions of the oral history resources available to them.

In Indiana, the Oral History Roundtable has been formed, an organization of individuals and institutions throughout the state proposing to exchange information about their respective oral history collections and act as a clearinghouse of information for new programs in Indiana. With this intent, they have held workshops; put out a quarterly newsletter, *The Recorder*; and published *A Survey of Oral History Collections in Indiana*. The State Library has been steadily expanding its oral history files since 1967, and hopes in the future to institute some sort of central bibliographical filing system of oral history collections throughout the state.

This and similar projects seem to point the way toward a more cooperative use of oral history materials. So far, the beginnings of extensive interlibrary loan arrangements have been few. The reason for this has been seen by some as the "custodial mentality" of oral historians, but is more likely a function of the early stages of development of many programs today. The amount of time, qualified personnel, and money needed to transform the oral history interview into a finished manuscript has kept many programs entirely involved in processing duties. Variations in legal restrictions have presented a further problem. But as greater numbers of these oral history centers mature, there will undoubtedly emerge a more cooperative attitude which will benefit researchers, historians, and oral history alike.

Published Bibliographies

There are other published bibliographies and guides. One is *Oral History in the United States: A Directory*, written by Gary Shumway and published in 1971 by the Oral History Association. This lists all established oral history programs known in the United States at that time, with summary surveys of their holdings, the size of their collections, and how researchers can use transcripts of interest to them. Due to the enormous growth and expansion of the number of oral history projects in the country over the last few years, though, Shumway's directory is unfortunately now incomplete. A new comprehensive guide entitled *Oral History Collections*, edited by Alan Meckler and Ruth McMullin, was published by Bowker in 1975. Oral history programs are indexed both geographically and by subjects in their collections.

Either or both of these books would be valuable to have in an oral history office for user reference and an in-office survey of the holdings of other programs. They would help one find other oral history centers that are collecting material on similar subjects. Through correspondence, one could expand the number of people served by a collection or at least have their lists available to those researching such topics.

Additional Repositories

By establishing efforts along many of the previously mentioned lines, an oral history office can ensure that users will quickly be able to find what they need and that information about the collection will get out to other oral history centers and the interested public. Another excellent means of making sure memoirs are available is to negotiate an agreement with a public library or an historical research library whereby one sends them duplicate copies of the office's oral history tapes. It is best to choose as a repository some library or historical society which has facilities to house historical materials and regular users' hours. Such an arrangement will greatly aid one in any efforts to widely disseminate an oral history collection.

Microfilming

Another similar possibility is having transcripts put on microfiche. The number of possible users can be infinitely multiplied in this way. Microfilming Corporation of America (MCA) presently has contracts with a small number of institutions to micropublish their oral history collections and advertise their availability in an annual catalog. The use of microfilming systems presents enormous new possibilities for the distribution and accessibility of oral history material and, indeed, may someday help to offset the costs of interview processing. Hopefully, the generally cooperative attitude of those narrators who have agreed to be interviewed will ensure that a sufficient number of them will also be willing to participate to make microfilming a successful means of dissemination. Many may have fears about nationwide distribution of their memoirs or feel that royalties should belong to them, even though they will probably be minimal.

Microfilming presents some potential problems that an oral history program should be aware of from the start. You should consider participating in the MCA project early on so that legal releases may be worded to include authorization to micropublish an interview. The suggested legal release format of MCA authorizes an oral history program to secure and renew copyright to an oral history memoir and contains a clause by which the narrator agrees to waive rights to any royalties the oral history program might receive through sales. It should also authorize the right to edit, as MCA insists that their lawyers read all material and be permitted to delete (edit) any portions which may be considered "offensive or libelous." Unless the legal release form used by one's office contains a waiver clause broad enough to cover such publishing and use as microfilming entails, the narrator will retain his/her right to such use and the royalties therefrom. Figure 44 shows a sample legal release covering all such contingencies encountered in the microfilming process.

One advantage of sending transcribed interviews to MCA for micropublishing is that they will compile an index of proper names for each memoir. Their processing (reading, indexing, microfiching) is supposed to be complete in 90 days, once they have received enough material to fill a 35-mm reel from which to work. For an oral history program with a small staff, this indexing source can be a help.

The multiple-access index that MCA has been planning to compile will also prove highly advantageous to participating oral history programs. Although this has been in process for several years and its status remains uncertain at present, it is hoped that it will be completed in the near future. Historians, archivists, students, and others will then be able to search memoirs in three ways: by narrator's names, by the subjects covered in the interviews, and by the names of people discussed therein. Such a central clearinghouse of oral history material would be one of the most valuable ways of disseminating an oral history collection. When it is in usable form, the MCA index will provide great dividends by making historical resources accessible on a nationwide scale. For further information, write to:

Director of Information
Microfilming Corporation of America
21 Harristown Road
Glenrock, New Jersey 07452

Publicity

Many oral history programs, especially younger and smaller ones, need to inform and stimulate the public as well as serve it with finder's aids. Publicizing what one has is an important part of the larger job of dissemination; without it, the best catalogs and indexes may get little use.

_____ Giant City Library _____

For and in consideration of the participation by *Giant City Library* in any programs involving the dissemination of tape-recorded memoirs and oral history material for publication, copyright, and other uses, I hereby release all right, title, or interest in and to all of my tape-recorded memoirs to *Giant City Library* and declare that they may be used without any restriction whatsoever and may be copyrighted and published by the said *Library*, which may also assign said copyright and publication rights to serious research scholars.

In addition to the rights and authority given to you under the preceding paragraph, I hereby authorize you to edit, publish, sell and/or license the use of my Oral History memoir in any other manner which the *Giant City Library* considers to be desirable and I waive any claim to any payments which may be received as a consequence thereof by the *Library*.

PLACE *Giant City,*
       Oklahoma.
DATE *2|21|75*

Mary Whitefeather
(Interviewee)

Martha Vanness
(for *Giant City Library*)

Fig. 44. A sample legal release form for a micropublishing project.

There are many ways to inform the public about an oral history collection, and the best approach undoubtedly depends on local or special circumstances. But obviously it helps to attract attention in local media, including newspapers, magazines, radio, and television. Oral history memoirs are a natural subject for feature stories in a hometown newspaper; invite local reporters to scan the collection. Some oral history centers supply tapes for regular radio broadcasting of a "voices of history" program. Such publicity not only educates the reading and listening public about oral history in general and one's own work in particular, but it often stimulates persons to volunteer as narrators or helpers.

Another approach is to reach the public by providing various services to local organizations and groups. These can range from giving addresses or playing tapes in school classrooms and at club meetings to providing training or advice on interviewing to interested groups. While such activities may consume valuable time, they invariably widen the public knowledge and appreciation of what one is doing, and thus enhance the prospects for increasing the number of patrons.

School teachers might appreciate an opportunity to assign their students to some special research on local history. Tell them about your collection and invite them to send students.

Wider dissemination can come from announcements in scholarly journals, state organization newsletters, convention meetings, popular magazines, and other regional or national media. Encourage reporters and magazine editors to write news stories about your work, or submit your own articles for publication.

Once one embarks on a publicizing campaign, he/she is likely to discover that additional opportunities and requests tend to follow in rapid and gratifying order.

Recording This Work

When a transcript has been cataloged, make copies for MCA and any additional chosen repositories and mark the appropriate boxes on the INTERVIEW DATA SHEET. Extra spaces on that sheet have been provided for other dissemination efforts undertaken, such as a radio program or the compilation of a book catalog of one's collection. Those boxes should also be filled in at the appropriate time. A full record of the uses to which a memoir has been put should be maintained on the INTERVIEW DATA SHEET. Figure 45 is an INTERVIEW DATA SHEET showing that all work on the Johnson interviews has been completed and recorded.

EXERCISE 8: INDEXING A PRACTICE MEMOIR

Following the instructions in Step 7: Serving Users, prepare a proper name and subject index for the memoir edited in Exercise 6.

Tri-County Historical Society

INTERVIEW DATA SHEET

This section is to be completed by the Interviewer.

NARRATOR _Harold S. Johnson_ ADDRESS _1127 38th Street, Indianapolis, Indiana_ PHONE _643-8812_

BIRTHDATE _4/12/08_ BIRTHPLACE _Brockington, Tennessee_ INTERVIEWER _Jane Rogers_ PHONE _342-4461_

DATE(S) & PLACE OF INTERVIEW(S) _7/14/75_ _7/20_ _7/24_ _8/3_ _Narrator's Home_

COLLATERAL MATERIAL Yes [X] No [ ] TERMS _Open_

This section is for office use. Write the date in the larger columns and check the smaller ones to record each process.

TAPES	Received & Labeled	Collaterals Filed	Transcribing Begun	No. of Pages	Total Time	Catalogued	Audited	Editing Begun	Total Time	Review To Narrator	Returned	Reread	Preface	Final Typing Begun	Text Finished	Index, Table of Contents	Proofread	Corrected	Transcript Sent	Transcript Returned	Tape Sent	Tape Returned	Shelf Copy	Narrator's Copy	State Library	NUOMC	Microfilm	Radio	book catalog listing
1	7-22-75 ✓	✓	10/20/75 ✓	37	8½ hrs		✓	12-3-75	10¾	1-7-76	✓	✓	✓	2-21-76	✓	✓	✓	✓	3-11-76		12-4-76		✓	✓	✓	✓	✓	✓	✓
2	7-22-75		10/22/75	34	8 hrs		✓	12-5-75	9		✓	✓	✓		✓		✓	✓	"		"		✓	✓	✓	✓	✓	✓	✓
3	8-9-75 ✓		10/24/75	38	8½ hrs		✓	12-6-75	10 hrs		✓	✓							"		"		✓	✓	✓	✓	✓	✓	✓
4	"		10/25/75	14	3¾ hrs		✓	12-10-75	4½		✓	✓							"		"		✓	✓	✓	✓	✓	✓	✓
5	"		10/25/75	36	8¼ hrs		✓	12-10-75	19		✓	✓							"		"		✓	✓	✓	✓	✓	✓	✓

Fig. 45. A completed Interview Data Sheet.

EXERCISE 9: DISSEMINATING ORAL HISTORY

Develop a plan for disseminating information about an existing or planned oral history collection in your area.

a. Main repository for the collection:
b. Additional repository(ies)?
c. Additional card catalog(s) or union catalog?
d. Ideas for local press news and features:
e. Ideas for radio and television promotion:
f. Other listings (*NUCMC*, microfilming, etc.):

V

Managing Oral History

W hether launching an ambitious full-scale oral history program or simply pursuing an interest that may or may not grow, there are some basic principles and guidelines of administration, staffing, and equipping that merit careful attention.

Equipment

The first decision, and a perennial issue among oral historians, is whether to employ reel-to-reel or cassette recorders and tape. Both have their virtues and failings. Most oral history programs that have been active for some time began with reel-to-reel equipment because that was what was available at the time. It is awkward and expensive to shift modes, which probably explains why the majority of programs still use reels today. Tape reels and reel-to-reel equipment are more expensive and bulky than their cassette competitors, but they also offer better sound fidelity. Improvements in cassette technology and the development of satisfactory cassette transcribing equipment make it a preferred choice today. Cassette tapes and recorders are much simpler, more convenient, and more economical for interviewing purposes, and new product lines of cassette transcribers are quite satisfactory for office use. Another advantage of cassettes is the ability to prevent mistaken erasures once an interview has been recorded. By removing the two small plastic tabs near the ends in the back of the cassette, one effectively locks out the recording function.

Recorders should be mechanically dependable, economical, simple to operate, and portable. Experience has shown that the sound reproduction and mechanical dependability of cassette machines retailing for less than $40 is poor, making the purchase of such equipment a bad investment. On the other hand, it is not necessary to purchase the most expensive recorders, which cost $150 or more. Basic features to seek are the battery/AC power option; standard controls (playback volume, play, record, rewind, and fast-forward functions); end-of-tape alarm; automatic input volume control; and remote microphone. Built-in microphones, which are featured on some equipment, are convenient but inferior in recording quality, because they pick up motor vibrations. Other useful but unnecessary features are a rechargeable power pack, tape counter, and record/battery level indicator.

In recent years manufacturers have developed greatly improved cassette transcribing equipment, virtually eliminating the risks of tape jamming and breakage. Electronic and dictating equipment manufacturers offer transcribers for retail prices ranging from $250 to $600. Basic features to consider are a comfortable earphone or headset, variable speed control, stop/play/rewind foot pedal, fast-forward function, built-in speaker, and tape counter.

If one is operating on a slender budget, Sony Corporation offers a tape recorder (Sony TC-70) that can be used for transcribing purposes as well as recording. It has a special review control which enables back spacing while still in the play mode. While lacking the sound fidelity, convenience, and durability of transcribers, it nevertheless can serve a dual purpose for beginners, and it costs less than $100.

Office style typewriters are needed for transcribing. While electric machines may be preferable over manuals, the only basic feature to seek is triple-spacing. Also, cloth ribbons are more economical than carbon ribbons.

Transcribers ordinarily are equipped with lightweight earphones rather than headsets. Some people prefer these, but others find them uncomfortable or of inferior quality for precise listening. High quality headsets ($25 to $50 each) may be purchased in such a case.

Storage equipment will become an issue for any fast-growing oral history office. Equipment and even tapes can be stored in simple metal storage cabinets, though specialized tape storage equipment is also available at a higher cost. In either event, it is important to store tape in a metal cabinet in order to reduce chances of damage from magnetic fields. Vertical file cabinets can store transcripts and other materials in process. Standard library shelving and archival containers are the proper way to store finished memoirs and collateral materials.

Supplies

It is unwise to save money by purchasing off-brand or inferior recording tape. Not only will sound fidelity be inferior but the risk of breakage, jamming, and deterioration will be greater. Cassette tapes are available in lengths of 30,

60, 90, and 120 minutes. In the experience of most oral history offices, the 30-minute length is inadequate and the 120-minute tape has a dangerous habit of jamming.

Other incidental supplies are typing and carbon paper, ruled note pads, and plenty of red pens or pencils for editing. For transcribing one can use inexpensive but durable typing paper. The final typescript should be on high quality, heavy nonacidic paper.

Protecting Tapes and Equipment

While good quality tapes and recording equipment are durable, one must exercise care in safeguarding them from loss, malfunction, and deterioration. It is prudent (albeit expensive) to make duplications of the tapes, storing the master tape in a secure place and using the copy for all processing activities and patron requests. Tapes should be stored in the proper environment, which is the comfort, 70°-level of temperature and a range of 50 percent humidity. Experts disagree whether tapes should be stored flat or on edge; in either case keep them in a clean metal cabinet to minimize the risks of dust contamination and magnetic field damage. Rewind all tapes periodically (at least annually) in order to prevent warping and other strains that might distort the recorded voices.

Special care should be exercised with all tapes and transcripts that are closed or carry any restrictions as to patron use. They should be kept in a secure area, with access only by staff members who understand and observe strict rules governing their use.

Tape recorders and transcribers require careful use and regular maintenance. Equipment that is not in use should be protected from dust. Every few weeks the recording head and cassette housing should be cleaned with a cotton swab dipped in isopropyl alcohol. Periodically a head demagnetizer should be used to remove residual magnetic impulses that can impair the quality of the recording.

Office Files

Every program will have its distinctive filing system, but there are some general categories and common sense ideas that can help a new office get started. Some form of *prospects file* (preferably three-by-five-inch cards) is the best way to keep track of prospective narrators. The tapes (ideally, separate files for masters and duplicates) are best filed alphabetically by narrator's surname, though some programs arrange tapes in chronological order of production, by project, or by some numbering system. Tape containers should be labeled to simplify filing and retrieving. As soon as transcribing begins, a vertical file of *transcripts-in-process* will be needed, arranged according to the tape filing system. Collateral materials from interviews may be stored in a vertical file or in archival containers. Many oral history programs maintain an *interview information file* for their collections. Data cards or forms similar to the INTERVIEW DATA SHEET are filed alphabetically by narrator either in a large (five-by-eight-inch) card file or a loose-leaf binder. This file provides basic information about each interview and also a record of processing steps completed. It is an important tool for efficient and responsible office management. Finished transcripts (at least one master set and one circulating set) are often filed alphabetically in conventional book shelving, though a numerical cataloging system is also convenient. Basic finder's aids include a shelf list of three-by-five-inch card descriptions of each memoir in the collection, plus a cross-referenced narrator and subject card catalog (accompanied by a typed file—authority file—of main entry headings).

Staff

Many oral history programs must depend either partly or wholly on part-time volunteers rather than employed professionals. This produces serious problems of overall direction, planning, training, standardized procedures, and continuity, but it also raises possibilities for tapping community resources and enthusiasm. Many service clubs and other local organizations encourage members to perform volunteer duties. It is wise to solicit recruits from these sources and then screen them carefully to get a cadre of dependable volunteers. Even then there will probably be some attrition in the ranks.

Training volunteers is a time-consuming activity that can be more time and trouble than it's worth if one fails to get much volunteer effort in return. Pep talks and a bit of badgering are often necessary. Not everyone has the ability to interview effectively, no matter how much training they receive. Try to persuade such persons to get involved in transcribing, editing, or some other related activity.

While there are many distinct steps in the oral history process, it is desirable to have the same person perform more than one step, if he/she has the proper training. For example, the functions of transcriptionist and editor can be combined in one person whose growing familiarity with that particular memoir will likely result in higher quality and greater efficiency. In some cases, it is possible to have the same person follow through on a memoir all the way from interviewing to final processing, except for an outside reviewer. This not only improves the product but it may instill a sense of proprietary enthusiasm in that staff member.

In recruiting and screening transciptionists, it is helpful to devise a simple fifteen-minute transcribing test. This not only measures an applicant's speed and skill but also gives him/her a trial taste of what the work will be like.

Training staff members involves more than lecturing on the technical aspects of the job. It also includes dialogue or informal seminars on ethical and other less precise matters, and—most importantly—practical or "laboratory" experience. One can devise simple training exercises like the ones in this book as experiential activities for each staff member. Of course, these require follow-up evaluation and individual monitoring, but they accomplish much more in effective training than lecturing. If one is training interviewers, he/she naturally will concentrate on that phase of the process, but even interviewers should get at least a taste of transcribing and editing so that they will be sensitive to the complex tasks that follow their work.

Budget

There are too many variables among oral history programs to provide a model or minimum budget for beginners. Some groups may need to purchase recording equipment and others may not; some may depend entirely on volunteer labor, others may be obligated or able to employ professionals.

It is possible, however, to tailor a budget knowing certain facts. Equipment costs can be estimated as follows:

Cassette tape recorder	$ 75 (range $ 50–$150)
Cassette transcriber	$400 (range $250–$500)
Typewriter	$150 (range $ 75–$500)

The usual cost for cassette recording tape is $2 per running hour. Costs of other supplies such as typing paper can be calculated according to local conditions and needs.

The following table gives an approximate idea of the work involved in oral history interviewing. It is based on one hour's worth of tape-recorded interview.

Estimated Labor to Produce and Process One Hour Interview

Getting Ready	5 hours
Interviewing	2 hours
Transcribing (24–40 pages)	8 hours
Auditing	2 hours
Editing	8 hours
Finishing Touches	7 hours
Related Tasks	8 hours
	40 hours

While actual experiences will vary considerably according to total length of the interview and other variables, the above estimate represents a reasonably typical case. Actual costs can be estimated by multiplying the number of hours by hourly labor costs for each step that cannot be performed with volunteer help.

Another useful but crude rule of thumb is that it costs from $7 to $10 for every page of transcript produced. This figure includes labor and material costs. Assuming that a typical one-hour interview would yield 30 pages of transcript, one might calculate that total labor and materials costs for processing a one-hour interview would be between $210 and $300.

The high cost of oral history requires prudent management, as much streamlining as possible, and also some professional judgment about priorities. Since the heaviest costs come with processing tapes into transcripts, one can stretch a budget by screening all tapes and deciding which ones merit the investment of transcribing and editing. Every oral history program has its share of poor interviews which do not warrant expensive processing.

Funds to support an oral history budget can come from many sources. At least some continuing institutional support (from a university, library, historical society, and so on) is virtually essential, in order to assure stable effort during the lag (one year or even longer) between starting work and having a product (finished transcripts) to demonstrate its worth. Beyond this steady support oral history programs are eligible to receive foundation and other special grants to expand their activities. It also is possible to enter into contractual agreements with corporations and public and private agencies whereby one conducts a special oral history project in return for complete or partial financial subsidy.

Establishing Priorities

One danger of any volunteer operation is lack of direction. Some central individual or perhaps an advisory committee must set priorities not only on whom to interview but which tapes to process first, how to stretch limited budgets, and how to delegate tasks efficiently. This overall direction also applies to monitoring quality control over every phase of the work, supervising each staff member's activities, and adhering to the highest ethical and legal standards. Among the ethical and legal concerns of the office are the following:

1. That one fully understands copyright law and communicates it to staff members as well as narrators. This means that everyone involved be informed about their rights and responsibilities and that the manager has access to legal or professional advice concerning copyright, libel, slander, and so on.

2. That staff members always explain the program's purpose fully to narrators, and that narrators are afforded all reasonable rights and privileges, including the opportunity to review edited copy.

3. That one ensures safety and security for the collection of tapes, transcripts, and collateral materials, particularly those that carry restrictions as to use.

4. That one is equally scrupulous in securing the working files and off-the-record data collected.

5. That all of the transcribing and editing performed by the program be motivated and guided by the principle of fidelity to the spoken word, as explained in chapter III.

Professional Awareness and Assistance

Even the smallest oral history venture needs to address itself to matters of common professional concern, and it will gain from such attention. Joining the Oral History Association (Executive Secretary, OHA, North Texas State University, Denton, Texas 76203) and participating in its activities is the most important way to accomplish this. The OHA is an organization of both full-time professionals and amateurs; its *Newsletter*, other publications, and annual meetings are an invaluable source of professional enrichment and comradeship. Though it has grown rapidly in recent years, OHA still is a friendly group, and its meetings have an informal atmosphere that makes even the newest recruit feel comfortable. In recent years, its annual National Colloquium has featured a preliminary training workshop for novices.

Corresponding with other oral historians is another means of professional association. In some states, practitioners have established information organizations that provide periodic and convenient opportunities for sharing ideas.

Develop a working library of oral history materials, including technical publications, articles, exemplary books based on oral history, and reference works. The bibliography in this book is a good place to begin selecting library acquisitions.

The OHA has adopted a statement of "Goals and Guidelines" which can serve any oral history program as an operating creed. The statement follows.

Oral History Association

Goals and Guidelines

The Oral History Association recognizes Oral History for what it is—a method of gathering a body of historical information in oral form usually on tape. Because the scholarly community is involved in both the production and use of oral history, the Association recognizes an opportunity and an obligation on the part of all concerned to make this type of historical source as authentic and as useful as possible.

Guidelines for the Interviewee:

1. The person who is interviewed should be selected carefully and his wishes must govern the conduct of the interview.

2. Before undertaking a taped interview for the purpose stated above, the interviewee (or narrator) should be clear in his mind regarding mutual rights with respect to tapes and transcripts made from them. This includes such things as: seal privilege, literary rights, prior use, fiduciary relationships, the right to edit the tape transcriptions, and the right to determine whether the tape is to be disposed of or preserved.

3. It is important that the interviewee fully understand the project, and that in view of costs and effort involved, he assumes a willingness to give useful information on the subject being pursued.

Guidelines for the Interviewer:

1. It should be the object of the interviewer to gather information that will be of scholarly usefulness in the present and the future. The interviewer who is collecting oral history materials for his own individual research should always bear in mind this broader objective.

2. In order to obtain a tape of maximum worth as a historical document, it is incumbent upon the interviewer to be thoroughly grounded in the background and experience of the person being interviewed, and, where appropriate and if at all feasible, to review the papers of the interviewee before conducting the interview. In conducting the interview an effort should be made to provide enough information to the interviewee to assist his recall.

3. It is important that all interviews be conducted in a spirit of objectivity and scholarly integrity and in accordance with stipulations agreed upon.

Guidelines for Sponsoring Institutions:

1. Subject to meeting the conditions as prescribed by interviewees, it will be the obligation of sponsoring institutions to prepare easily usable tapes and/or accurate typed transcriptions, and properly to identify, index, and preserve such oral history records for use by the scholarly community, and to state clearly the provisions that govern their use.

A Final Word

A persistent and central theme of this book has been its emphasis upon the complexity and gravity of oral history. Collecting, processing, and disseminating this distinctive historical resource is a serious business, and must not be undertaken lightly or casually. The human memory is a scarce resource; we cannot afford to tap it frivolously or squander it on ill-prepared interviewing. Civil liberties are precious rights that must not be jeopardized by unethical or unscrupulous practices. High standards in both the historical and librarian professions obligate the oral historian to perform all tasks responsibly and diligently. Oral history's substantial investments in time, energy, and money require every practitioner to work hard and economize. The inevitable presence of historical trivia in any memoirs collection compels us to make painful decisions about priorities.

While summarizing and thus reasserting these sobering thoughts, the authors wish to close on a lighter and more encouraging note. First, we believe that proficiency in any oral history skill can be learned. It may take careful reading and repeated practice, but one can master the intricacies of indexing, the concepts of editing, and the craft of interviewing. It *can* be done, or the authors would not have written a book telling how to do it.

Second, the practicing oral historian will quickly discover significant and often unexpected rewards in this work. There is the pleasure in learning about one's own community, the nation, or the human condition generally. There is the joy of new friends; one of oral history's serendipities is the warm friend-ships that grow out of interviewing. There is the incalculable gratification that comes from unearthing unique historical data. No matter its modest scope or humble substance, any oral history memoir adds something to our treasury of preserved history. By contributing to society's collective self-knowledge, one gains a heightened sense of individual worth.

EXERCISE 10: CHECKLIST FOR PURCHASING EQUIPMENT

If you are considering the purchase of cassette recording and transcribing equipment, take this checklist along when you shop.

Tape Recorders	Model #1	Model #2	Model #3	Model #4
Battery/AC power option				
Standard controls				
End-of-tape alarm				
Automatic input volume control				
Built-in microphone				
Rechargeable power pack				
Tape counter				
Record/battery level indicator				
Price				

Transcribers	Model #1	Model #2	Model #3	Model #4
Comfortable earphone				
Variable speed control				
Foot pedal: stop/play				
rewind				
Fast-forward function				
Built-in speaker				
Tape counter				
Price				

EXERCISE 11: MANAGING ORAL HISTORY

Following the advice in chapter V, plan the management aspects of an existing or proposed oral history program in your locality.

a. Equipment inventory and budget
b. Supplies inventory and budget
c. Staff positions (both paid and volunteer)
d. Specific goals and priorities

EXERCISE 12: INVENTORY OF ORAL HISTORY PROJECTS AND RESOURCES

Make an inventory of existing and planned oral history projects in your locality, and identify possible topics and resources.

a. Existing oral history projects (identify and describe)
b. Planned oral history projects (identify and describe)
c. Topics and special activities particularly appropriate to my locality
d. Potential sources of volunteer assistance
e. Potential sources of financial assistance
f. Potential sources for narrators
g. Most likely depository(ies) for tapes and transcripts
h. Strategy and schedule for planning and conducting oral history project

Appendixes

APPENDIX A

Glossary

Accession—a memoir newly received by an oral history office. Many programs periodically issue a list of accessions to inform users and as a public relations gesture.

Audit/Auditor—to listen simultaneously to the tape and read the rough transcript, correcting transcribing errors and omissions in order to prepare a verbatim transcript ready for editing.

Authority File or List—a record of the exact form of each heading and the references leading to it in a particular catalog. If on cards, it is called an authority file, each heading being listed on a separate card; if on sheets, it is called an authority list.

Book Catalog—a catalog in the form of a book.

Card Catalog—a catalog consisting of cards.

Cataloging—the indexing of an entire oral history collection.

Collateral Material—personal materials of the narrator such as scrapbooks, photographs, and newspaper clippings which contribute to the information given in an interview.

Descriptor—a subject heading under which a memoir is cataloged.

Dictionary Catalog—a catalog in which cards are interfiled in one alphabet with both main entry and subject cards.

Edit/Editor—to work on the audited transcript for the purpose of producing the rough draft of the final copy, being certain that the edited transcript has clarity, is punctuated, and worded to reflect the formal or informal tone of the interview; reads smoothly; and maintains the individuality of the speakers.

Editing Symbols—standardized marks used to indicate what changes are made and where when auditing, editing, and reviewing a transcript.

Entry—the complete description about any item, a bibliographical entity, in a catalog.

Final Typing—the typing of the edited, reviewed, and reread transcript to produce the copy which will be duplicated for bound memoirs or from which type will be set for printing the pages for the bound memoir.

Headset/Earphone—listening devices which come with the transcriber and which the transcriptionist places on his/her head or into the ears.

Index—an alphabetical list of names, places, topics giving reference to the pages on which they are mentioned in a transcript. Usually found at the back of a transcript. In addition, a tape may be indexed by time segments rather than pages. (See also cataloging.)

Interview Contents—a table of contents or index of a tape summarizing the topics covered as they occur in an oral history interview. Usually divided according to time segments.

Interview Data Sheet—a form providing basic biographical and related information for each oral history narrator; also a work sheet to be used in the oral history office by which the status of a memoir can be quickly ascertained.

Interviewer—a trained oral historian who conducts interviews with narrators (subjects).

Interviewer's Comments—postinterview observations by an interviewer of the interview setting, likely value of the interview, and veracity of the narrator.

Interviewer's Notes and Word List—a list of all proper names and unfamiliar terms made by the interviewer with the narrator's assistance and for the convenience and accuracy of the transcriptionist; also includes notes about passages which may be hard to understand or are to be kept in confidence.

Legal release—see Release, legal.

Memoir—an oral history transcript, representing all of the interviews by one interviewer with one narrator.

Microfiche—a sheet of microfilm (a film upon which oral history memoirs are photographed greatly reduced in size), usually measuring four by six inches, upon which transcript pages are reproduced in serial form.

Narrator/Interviewee/Subject—a person whose eyewitness historical recollections are the object of an oral history interview.

Proofreading—a reading done by two persons, one reading the rough final transcript and the other checking the final typed copy against it.

Release, legal—an open release is one in which the narrator has fully released his/her rights to the interview material and researchers may freely read, cite, and quote it. A restricted memoir has a release which makes some restrictions on usage: that the narrator prefers not to be quoted or that he/she wants certain portions to remain confidential. A closed memoir has a release which states that the material will not be available for use for a certain period of time.

Reread—a check of the edited transcript by the editor or another staff member for clarity and semantic flow before it goes to the narrator for review; also, a review for the same reason by the editor after the transcript is returned by the narrator and before it is typed in final form.

Review—the narrator's reading of the edited transcript to ascertain that it reflects his/her intended meaning, during which clarifications, corrections, additions, explanations, and (a minimum of) deletions can be made.

Rules of Style—the guidelines used in processing to ensure that the format of abbreviations, numbers, punctuation, and so on in the finished memoir is consistent with common and/or comprehensible usage.

SEE Reference—a reference which directs the researcher to look under an equivalent main term because the chosen subject heading is not used in a catalog or index.

SEE ALSO Reference—a reference which gives subject headings for corresponding, comparable, and related material, in alphabetical order in a catalog or index.

Shelf List—a list or file of cards in the order in which the transcripts are shelved, usually alphabetically by narrators' surnames.

Subject Card Catalog—a catalog which groups cards so that transcripts which discuss the same subject are listed next to each other, as opposed to a narrator card catalog, which lists transcripts alphabetically by narrator.

Table of Contents—a list of the divisions of a transcript in subject matter, arranged in the sequence in which they appear in the transcript and listing the pages on which they begin.

Tracing System—the notes needed to locate or trace other, related cards filed in a catalog. Composed of three parts: (1) an authority file, (2) the records of added entries made on unit cards, behind which an overtyped copy of the unit card is filed, (3) the cross-reference notations (x and xx) made on the backs of the guide cards in the subject card catalog.

Transcribe/Transcriptionist—to present in typewritten or handwritten form an accurate and complete account of the taped interview

Transcriber—the machine which plays the tape during transcription

Transcript—the typed or handwritten account of an interview; referred to as the rough transcript until it is audited; the audited transcript until edited, and so forth.

APPENDIX B

Rules of Style

Preface

Style refers to printing style or format. A transcript which follows recognized or at least consistent and understandable standards of style is easier to read. Transcriptionists and auditors should be familiar with these *Rules of Style* so that transcripts will need a minimum of change during editing. Editors have final responsibility for applying the rules. Final typists will find it easier to understand what they are typing when they too are familiar with the rules.

These particular rules do not cover the most elementary rules of grammar. They do include commonly encountered and particularly troublesome style problems. One will probably have to use additional resources such as a book on style or grammar to decide how to handle some problems. But because the historian is working with casual, spoken language and most style resources are written primarily for formal language, one may not find the solutions needed. However, novels with plenty of dialogue or books based on oral history interviews may prove to be good resources.

When it is difficult to find a ready-made answer, consult with co-workers and use personal judgment to work out a solution. Follow existing rules as closely as possible so that the chosen form of expression will be recognizable and understandable to the reader.

I. Abbreviations
  A. The important basic rule for using abbreviations is that any abbreviation appearing in the transcript must be a reflection of its use by the speaker. *Do not abbreviate what he/she said.* Therefore, words like the following must always be fully expressed in an oral history transcript even though their abbreviations are commonly used and understood in writing.
    1. "et cetera," "versus," "okay"
    2. "Street," "Avenue," "Building"
    3. words that express weights and measurements like "ton," "foot"
  B. Abbreviations used by the speaker should be typed in the transcript in order to accurately reflect the interview (except years, see Section VI., E.). However, some abbreviations will require clarifying explanation.
    1. Abbreviations such as the following are so commonly used in both speech and writing that they can be understood from context and need no explanation. (Note how the apostrophe is used.)

D.T.'s	a.w.o.l.	a.m.
K.O.'s	photos	p.m.
TB	cons	C.O.D.
Ph.D.	B.V.D.'s	I.O.

    2. Jargon or colloquialisms which are not generally familiar should be explained the first time they appear by inserting the meaning, within brackets, after the word. If the explanation requires more than a few words, an explanatory footnote should be used instead. (See instructions for footnotes in Section IV.)
        Con Con [Illinois Constitutional Convention of 1970]
        blackdamp [a concentration of carbon dioxide in a coal mine]
        on the q.t. [quietly; on the sly]
    3. Spoken abbreviations of the names of governmental agencies and social or business organizations which may not be immediately recognized by the average reader should be identified the first time they appear by inserting the full name, within brackets, after the word. Verify the official spelling and capitalization of the full name.
        CIO [Congress of Industrial Organizations]
        ITT [International Telephone and Telegraph]
        IOOF [International Order of Odd Fellows]
        DVR [Department of Vocational Rehabilitation]
    4. If the speaker uses an abbreviation but says the "of" or "and" which occurs in the full name, type it.
        U.S. of A.   AF of L   AT and T
    5. Some abbreviations always appear with periods, some don't.
        A.D.   B.C.   C.O.D.   a.m.   p.m.
        U.S.—but USA   U.N.
    When in doubt, follow the suggestion that periods are not necessary in abbreviations of three or more letters.
    6. When a decision is made on the style of any abbreviation, that form should be written on the editor's word list for easy reference in ensuring that it will appear in the same form throughout the transcript.

II. Brackets and Parentheses
    A. Brackets are used to indicate that the words within them were not on the tape.
        1. Brackets cannot be replaced with parentheses. If your typewriter does not have brackets, make them by typing the diagonal mark where the brackets would go and then draw in top and bottom lines with a fine point pen ⎾⏌ or leave an extra space and draw them [ ].
        2. Bracket major editorial insertions made to provide clarity.
            a. Major verbs, pronoun antecedents, and some explanatory words are bracketed.
            b. See Section I for use with Abbreviations.
            c. See Section V for use with Names.
    B. Parentheses are used to enclose typed notations of action or emotion. Make such explanatory notes telegraphic; capitalization and periods are not necessary.
        1. Action may consist of
            a. An interruption of taping—even those apparent from context.
                A: I found only a little . . . (phone rings, taping stopped and started again)
                Q: Before the phone rang and we stopped, you were telling me about your experience with the Salvation Army.
                — or —
                A: It's hard to remember. Turn that off a minute. (tape stops and starts again) It wasn't like I said. What really happened was that we all went.
            b. An interruption *not* obvious from context.
                A: Well, let me find that. (walks away and part of narrative is inaudible) . . . it shows how we worked.
                — or —
                A: That is here somewhere. (shuffles through papers)
        2. Audible expression of emotion
            (laughter) if both narrator and interviewer laughed
            (laughs) if speaker laughed—especially narrator
            (chuckles) if narrator chuckled as he/she spoke
            (weeps)
            (pounds fist on table)
            (pause) a *long* mid-sentence pause
        3. Do not use parentheses to enclose a speaker's parenthetical words. (See Section VIII, Punctuation.)

III. Capitalization
    A. Capitalize the first word in a sentence of related dialogue, of related thought, or of directly quoted material.
            I started to leave and, "Hey, Big Boy," she said, "come up and see me some time." I thought, "You bet I will."
            — or —
             Yes. This book says, "Our dialect word for whore is La Troiana" —T-R-O-I-A-N-A—"the Trojan woman, a term transmitted orally from a long series of generations by a non-literate people."

Note: when related dialogue, and so on, are interrupted and then resumed, the first word within the second set of quotation marks is not capitalized if it does not begin a new sentence.

B. Capitalize and separate with hyphens the letters of a word spelled out by a speaker (see the above example).

C. The first word of rules, axioms, slogans, or mottos should be capitalized. No quotation marks are needed; note the use of the comma.

> Our motto is, Be prepared.
> His favorite saying was, Better late than never.

D. Some geographical terms are capitalized, but only those that make reference to specific places. One can usually tell from context whether or not capitalization is needed.

E. Capitalize historical periods, important events, and documents.

> the Great Depression—but—the depression of the thirties
> the Roaring Twenties—but—the twenties
> the Middle Ages—but—medieval
> World War I—but—before the war and postwar
> the Great War [WWI]—note that this needs to be explained
> the Declaration of Independence

F. Religious terms

1. Capitalize the names of religious denominations and their adherents.

> Protestantism, a Protestant, the Protestant
> the Protestant Episcopal Church
> Catholicism, a Catholic, the Church of Rome
> Judaism, a Jew, Jewish, Reform Judaism,
> an Orthodox congregation

2. Capitalize the titles of sacred writings. Do not underline them.

> the Bible   the Talmud   the Koran

G. Trade names

1. Capitalize a trade name used to specify a specific brand. Notice that the article described by the trade name is not capitalized.

> We like Jello pudding.
> Make a Xerox copy.
> We have a Ford station wagon.

2. Do not capitalize trade names that have come to be considered common nouns when they are used as nouns.

> victrola   dictaphone
> corn flakes   kleenex

IV. Footnotes

Lengthy explanatory material should be placed in footnotes rather than in the body of the transcript. Explanatory material consists of definitions, information known about a subject which would help the reader understand an unclear passage, or explanation of the handling of something in the transcript. The narrator can add or delete explanatory footnotes during his/her review of the transcript.

A. All footnotes must be signed so the reader knows who is providing the information.
   1. The editor should sign (Ed.) or (Editor).
   2. Explanations added by the narrator should be signed with the narrator's name or initials: (Phyllis Diller) or (P.D.).

B. Use arabic numerals in the text to indicate that there is a footnote; do not use asterisks. Footnotes should appear on the page on which they are referenced in the text. Number them sequentially throughout the transcript.

C. Editors and final typists should be familiar with the style for footnotes (see figure 17).

V. Names, Titles

A. The proper forms of the names of agencies and organizations must be verified by the editor. If part of a name is omitted by a speaker, insert that part in brackets.

> the Illinois Central [Railroad]

B. Proper names and nicknames mentioned in an interview should be fully and officially identified, within brackets, the first time they appear.

> Mrs. [Elizabeth] Jones—use the woman's name, not her husband's.
> Mrs. [Elizabeth Smith] Jones—if the maiden name is of historical significance.
> John L. [Lewis], Ole John L. [Lewis], Mr. [John L.] Lewis—include the initial if it is important for identification.
> Fuzzy [Frank Long], [Frank] Fuzzy Long—the nicknames do not require quotation marks.

C. Capitalize the official titles of books and magazines and underline them. Capitalize and underline the parts of the names of newspapers that appear on their mastheads. Capitalize and underline the names of airplanes.

Words Into Type	Gone with the Wind
Newsweek	the Ladies Home Journal
The New York Times	the St. Louis Post-Dispatch
Air Force One	the Spirit of St. Louis

D. Capitalize and place in quotation marks the major words in the titles of plays, movies, and television programs.

> "The Boys in the Band"
> "Gone with the Wind"
> "To Tell the Truth"

VI. Numbers

A. General Rules
   1. Use *words* to express
      a. numbers *one through twenty*
      b. *round* numbers

> seventy, seven hundred, seventy million

      c. *approximate* numbers

         about twenty thousand seven hundred people

         oh, like twenty-five copies

         around twenty-three children

      d. *isolated numbers*—those that occur alone within a space of several lines of type

  2. Use *numerals* to express

      a. *numbers over twenty except* round, approximate, or isolated numbers

      b. *whole numbers* which occur *with fractions*

         The cat weighs 8½ pounds.

      c. numbers *in a series* and *comparable* numbers—those which all refer to the same thing

         There are children with 10, 12, 23, and 25 days of absence in this semester.

B. Special Cases

  1. Use *words* to express the *first group mentioned* when two groups of comparable numbers occur in a sentence.

      Of the women who applied, three were 18, two were 21, and thirty-three were over 40.

  2. Use *words* to express numbers which begin a sentence. It may be necessary to insert or rearrange words if a year or street address is mentioned. Brackets are not needed unless the inserted words might be of significance to the reader.

      "The year 1929 was bad" when "1929 was a bad year" was verbatim.

           — or —

      "At 2200 Elm Street" when "Twenty-two hundred Elm Street" was verbatim.

  3. Use *words* to express the *first of two numbers which appear together* and which might cause confusion if both were expressed in the same form. Note the use of the hyphen to indicate the compound adjectives.

      eight 1-inch pipes

      two 12-acre homesteads

      thirty-three 25-page pamphlets

  4. Use *numerals* for the first number in cases like the following (see F. 3 below).

      We needed 8 two-by-fours.

C. Addresses and Street Names

  1. Use *numerals* for street addresses.

      "2000 Elm Street" even if "two thousand Elm Street" was verbatim.

  2. Use *words* for the names of numbered streets or avenues unless three digits would be required.

      Fifth Avenue—not—5th Avenue

      Forty-second Street—not—42nd Street

           — but —

      101st Street—not—One hundred one (or first) Street

D. Ages follow the General Rules and Special Cases above.

E. Dates and Years

   1. Dates should be made immediately recognizable to the reader. Use the *common form*, January 1, 1970, when *both a day and year* are mentioned. "January the first, nineteen hundred and seventy" would never be used, even if "the" and "and" were verbatim.

   2. The *verbatim is acceptable when only a month and day are mentioned*. Use numerals to express the day.

        January 1   January 1st
        1 January   the 1st of January

   3. *Do not abbreviate years* even if that was verbatim; when typing the year, be sure to set it in the correct century.

        1961—not—'61

   4. Decades should be abbreviated when that is verbatim, but *use words*, not numerals.

        the fifties—not—the '50's
        the 1950's, if that was verbatim

F. Dimensions

   1. Express dimensions in *numerals*.

   2. Type "by" rather than "x" and leave a space before and after "by."

        20 by 45 feet—or—20 feet by 45 feet—whichever is verbatim

   3. If *no quantitative measurement* was mentioned, the dimensions are considered compound adjectives or nouns and are hyphenated. Express the numbers in *words* and type "-by-."

        The room was twenty-by-forty-five.
        A two-by-four held it in place.
        We bought 18 two-by-fours (see Special Cases VI. B. 4).

G. Fractions

   1. Use *words* to express *isolated fractions*. Type a hyphen between the numerator and the denominator.

        five-twentieths
        "The jar was one-half full"—but—"The jar was half full" if that is verbatim

   2. Use *numerals* to express *fractions used with whole numbers*. Type a diagonal line between the numerator and the denominator.

        The recipe called for 10 pounds of potatoes, 15 pounds of meat, and 2½ pounds of flour.

H. Money

   1. Use *words*

     a. when an amount of money *begins a sentence*.

        Six dollars and seventy-nine cents was too much.

     b. when it is an *isolated round amount* of either dollars or cents.

        The price was sixty dollars.
        I found seventy cents.

     c. when it is an *approximate amount*.

        It was in the vicinity of seven hundred fifty dollars.

     d. when either several *round all-dollar amounts* or several *all-less-*

than-a-dollar amounts appear in the sentence and are isolated, that is, no other amounts of money occur within a space of several lines.

> We took home those days ten dollars or twenty dollars; now it's one hundred dollars.
>
> The trinkets cost seventy-five to ninety cents.

2. Use *numerals*
   a. when it is *an isolated amount of dollars and cents*.
      > I earned $6.75.
   b. when a *round amount* appears with other amounts.
      > I gave him $50 and he gave me $21 in change.
3. Dollars and zero/cent columns.
   a. In the above example, decimal points and zeros are not used because neither amount requires them. In the following example, one amount includes cents, so the decimal point and zero/cents columns are included in the other amount as well.
      > I gave him $50.73 and he gave me $2.00 in change.
   b. In the following example, each amount has empty columns which are necessary to reflect the presence of those columns in the other amount.
      > I gave him $50.00 in bills and $0.23 in change, and he gave me my bag of groceries.

I. Percentages
1. Both *percent* and *per cent* are acceptable, but use one form consistently throughout a transcript. The percent symbol (%) is never acceptable.
2. Use *numerals* to express *exact* percentages.
   > It was 75 percent complete.
3. Use *words* to express *approximate* percentages.
   > I'd estimate the stadium was eighty percent full.

J. Ratios
1. Use *numerals* to express ratios.
2. Use the *hyphen*, with no spaces between it and the numerals it separates, to express the spoken "to." Note how the comma is used.
   > The vote was split, 12-18.
   >
   > Our class was divided, 21-47.

K. Time
1. Use *words* to express time if the narrator says "o'clock."
   > four o'clock Wednesday
   >
   > four-fifteen o'clock Wednesday
2. Use *numerals* for other expressions of time and type what is verbatim.
   > at 4:15 on Wednesday afternoon
   >
   > at 4:15 p.m. on Wednesday
   >
   > at 4:00 on Wednesday afternoon
   >
   > at 4:00 p.m. on Wednesday
   >
   > at 4:00 p.m. on Wednesday afternoon
3. If no indication of a.m. or p.m. is spoken, but one can tell from con-

text which is intended, insert the a.m. or p.m. No brackets are needed.

4. If one cannot tell from context whether morning or afternoon is intended, the transcriptionist should type a blank line or the editor should circle the time and make a note in the left margin for the narrator.

VII. Paragraphing

It is discouraging to have to read a full page of type that has no paragraphs. Transcriptionists should begin a new paragraph when there is a topical change. Editors should look carefully for places to divide a page that has no paragraphs.

A. A good place to begin a new paragraph when there is not a definite topical change is where the narrator takes a slightly different tack on the same topic. One can also listen to the tape to see if there is a sentence which is given particular emphasis by the speaker and which would be a good beginning sentence for a paragraph.

B. Ideal paragraph length for quick and easy reading is ten or twelve lines, but the overriding consideration in paragraphing is unification of thought.

C. On the other hand, avoid a page of unnecessarily short, choppy paragraphs.

D. Do not paragraph with each change of speakers in related dialogue. The following example is the correct style.

And he said, "Make them just a degree better than a hog sty." Somebody says, "Why? Why that kind of a house for men to live in that mine our coal? Why not make them more substantial?" And I says, "Right, that's right."

VIII. Punctuation

The commonly accepted rule for punctuating is that a sentence should contain no more punctuation than is required to insure clarity. But writers also use punctuation to indicate how a sentence should be read: where the reader should pause, what parts should be given emphasis.

Punctuation in a transcript has a dual purpose. It must be used both for clarity and for fidelity to the spoken word. This dual purpose may result in too much punctuation which would destroy clarity and damage readability. The confused reader would form a low opinion of the oral history transcript as historical source material.

Therefore, the commonly accepted rule in preparing a transcript is to use the minimum amount required to achieve both clarity and a sense of how the interview sounded. If some punctuation provided by the transcriptionist *must* be deleted by the editor to achieve clarity, punctuation used to convey sound may legitimately be sacrificed. But, first, try to find a way to *repunctuate* the sentence.

The following examples show a poorly punctuated bit of transcription and the editor's finished product.

> Now, of course, actually, at that time, being a patient in a state hospital, you were, your feelings were pretty much—and I know I can't speak from complete authority, but I think I know how they felt, and I'm relating what I thought it was like.

In the above example, the comma after the introductory word "Now" is necessary. It was apparent from listening to the tape, however, that the words "of course actually" were spoken as one entity, so the comma there was deleted. The comma after "at that time" is necessary to sentence construction; the comma after "hospital" is necessary. The comma after "you were" is necessary to show a change in phrasing. The dash is both necessary and a good bit of punctuation for that abrupt change in thought. The comma before "but" is necessary; the comma before "and" is not.

The edited sentence in the example below is better punctuated, but still hard to read.

> Now, of course actually, at that time, being a patient in a state hospital, you were, your feelings were pretty much—and I know I can't speak from complete authority, but I think I know how they felt and I'm relating what I thought it was like.

The following example shows a better solution achieved by deleting meaningless crutch words and a false start.

> Now, at that time, being a patient in a state hospital, your feelings were pretty much—and I know I can't speak from complete authority, but I think I know how they felt and I'm relating what I thought it was like.

The sentence still reflects the speaker's individuality: the introductory word, the qualifying way in which he speaks, and the essentially unchanged sentence construction. There is enough punctuation to provide clarity and to show the rhythm of speech.

This section on punctuation does not include the most commonly known rules. Refer to a grammar or style book as often as necessary to avoid using punctuation incorrectly or unnecessarily.

The rules that are included here cover points that are frequently asked about or incorrectly handled. Also included are special ways in which punctuation can be used in transcripts.

A. Apostrophe

1. Use the apostrophe to punctuate the forms of plural numbers and letters.

> the 1950's—but—the fifties
> B.V.D.'s   A.B.C.'s
> Are you up to the 125's on the list?

2. Use the apostrophe in most possessives, but omit it if common usage dictates.

> State's Attorney
> teachers college

3. Use the apostrophe to show the possessive form of inanimate objects.

> a week's wait   two weeks' vacation
> one dollar's worth   ten dollars' worth

B. Colon

   1. The colon means "that is" or "for example." Use it when those words are understood in a sentence.

   2. *Do not* use a colon when words such as "that is," "for example," "like," *were spoken.*

   3. Do not use a colon when a comma would suffice, but use it if a comma would cause confusion.

Wrong:	We needed everything like: food, water, shelter, medicine.
Correct but Poor:	We needed everything, food, water, shelter, medicine.
Correct and Better:	We needed everything: food, water, shelter, medicine.

C. Comma

   1. Commas are frequently overused by transcriptionists and editors. Be sure that a comma placed to convey a speaker's pause does not confuse the meaning of the typed sentence.

   2. A comma should not be used to convey sound if using it violates a common rule of punctuation and, thus, confuses the reader.

   3. Consider using other punctuation in place of the comma to convey sound. It may be necessary to use punctuation in ways discouraged by composition teachers, but ways which are nevertheless acceptable and understandable in a less formal context.

     a. Use the comma to indicate that a brief pause was made by the speaker and should be made by the reader. For pauses of longer duration, use the dash or three points of the ellipsis (see Sections VIII, D. and E. below). Decide which to use by listening to the tape.

     b. Use commas to indicate that what they punctuate is different, to a slight degree, from the rest of the sentence. This should be apparent either from context or from listening to the tape. Appositives and minor parenthetical material should be set off with commas when possible. See Section VIII, D. for how to use dashes to indicate a greater degree of difference. *Never* use parentheses for parenthetical material in a transcript.

D. Dash

   1. Dashes (—) are made by striking the hyphen key twice. Leave no space between the dash and the words around it.

   2. Use dashes in transcripts

     a. to set off an appositive, ordinarily set off by commas, when there are commas within the appositive.

Poor:	The town's dump, smelly, smoky, rat-infested, disease-spreading place, was his favorite haunt.
Better:	The town's dump—smelly, smoky, rat-infested, disease-spreading place—was his favorite haunt.

     b. to separate parenthetical material from the rest of a sentence.

Parenthetical material has no essential connection to the rest of the sentence in which it occurs. It is especially important to use dashes when the parenthetical material contains commas. *Never* use parentheses for this purpose.

> Poor: The town's dump, I used to play there as a child, so did my best friend, was adjacent to our farm.
>
> Better: The town's dump—I used to play there as a child, so did my best friend—was adjacent to our farm.

   c. to mark a sudden change in sentence construction.

> They were mostly—what's the word—aliens.

   d. to mark an unexpected change of thought.

> No one ever asked me that so I never told anyone about— you know, being chairman was a ticklish thing.

   e. to indicate a faltering or false start.

> No one was—they were all aliens.

   f. to indicate that related conversation or quoted material is interrupted by the speaker.

> Jerry said, "Let's go to the pizza parlor"—Jerry hates pizza so I knew something was up—"for your birthday treat."

(See also example under III, A.)

2. Use the dash to tell the reader that there was a longer pause than a comma would suggest, or that what follows it is of greater difference from the rest of the sentence than a comma would suggest. Length of pause and degree of difference are often simultaneously indicated. That could have been the case in b., c., d., e., and f. In a. above and the example below, however, there is no difference expressed, only pause.

> I think they felt pretty much as being incarcerated—like being locked up in a jail.

In the above example, the speaker paused dramatically to emphasize what he had said, and then he restated his point for emphasis.

E. Ellipsis

1. Points of ellipsis are made by striking the period three times, spacing between the periods.

2. The *three points* of ellipsis used alone indicate that the sentence was uncompleted because *the speaker was interrupted and not allowed to finish it.*

   a. This may be caused by an outside interruption.

> A: I found only a little . . . (phone rings, taping stopped and started again)
>
> Q: You were telling me about moving.

   b. This may occur when one speaker interrupts the other.

> A: We went to the theater . . .
>
> Q: Which theater?
>
> A: The Roxy theater. We went there and then to Mary's house.

In the above example, the narrator was stopped. In the following example, the narrator went right on talking despite the interrupting question. To show when the second question was asked, the three points of the ellipsis were used both before and after the question. Notice that the first word in the second part of the answer is not capitalized.

> Q: Who called you?
> A: It was Squirrely who . . .
> Q: Who is Squirrely?
> A: . . . called me about it. You know Squirrely—Max Bond.

3. *Four dots* (really a period immediately after the last word and then the three points of the ellipsis) are used to indicate that a well-begun sentence was left uncompleted and followed by a new sentence—not that a false start was made. *The speaker did not finish* it because he/she

   a. thought better of it and did not want to finish.
   b. did not know how to finish it so just quit.
   c. lost track of his/her thought and drifted to a stop.

   It indicates a pause *between sentences*, not mid-sentence as a dash would indicate.

   > A: Any other time I'd have helped someone like that, someone in trouble. This time, though, this guy was a real risk—jobless, poor job record—and we couldn't help. We just didn't feel. . . . Other times, though, we were able to help people. Our policy . . . (phone rings, taping stopped and started again)
   > Q: You were going to tell me . . .
   > A: Oh yes. Our policy was to check first and loan later.

F. Exclamation point
   1. *Use* the exclamation point to show that the speaker strongly emphasized a *sentence*. Use these sparingly so that they do not lose their impact upon the reader.
   2. *Don't use* the exclamation point within a sentence to indicate that a *word* was strongly emphasized. The following example shows incorrect usage.

      > It was so hot! in the house we couldn't stay.

      If only hot was emphasized, leave the sentence with only a period for punctuation. If the whole sentence was emphasized, but hot especially, use an exclamation point at the end of the sentence. Some narrators speak dramatically; but do not punctuate all indications of that characteristic or the exclamation mark will lose its dramatic effect.

G. Hyphen
   1. Use hyphens to separate letters when a speaker spells a word.

      > Her name is Susie Coy, C-O-Y. I think her name affected her personality.

   2. Use a hyphen between inclusive years unless the words and, to, or through are spoken.

      > Well, that all happened sometime between 1957–1961.
      > It was suppose to run 1975–1976.

3. Do not divide contractions (couldn't, aren't) at the ends of lines of type. If the whole word will not fit at the end of a line, type it all on the next line.

4. Hyphenated compound words require careful attention by transcriptionists, editors, and final typists.

   a. Deciding correctly whether or not to hyphenate a word is important. Be sure the meaning conveyed is the one the speaker intended.

      Did the speaker mean, "Lydia was a great-aunt to her" or "Lydia was a great aunt to her"?

      Were there "ten acre farms" or were they "ten-acre farms"?

      Do you want "two-dollar tickets" or "two dollar tickets"?

   b. Editors must circle the hyphen of a hyphenated word to alert final typists when it is inserted in editing or appears at the end of a line of type. Suppose "truck-farming" was divided during transcription and "truck-" was on one line and "farming" on the next. If the hyphen were not circled during editing, the final typist would be justified in typing "truckfarming" if the word came mid-line in the final copy.

   c. Transcriptionists and final typists must divide a hyphenated word only between the words.

      Suppose "truck-farming" does not all fit on a line. It cannot be divided "truck-farm-" on one line and "ing" on the next.

H. Quotations, Quotation Marks

  1. Use quotation marks to show a related conversation, a direct thought, or directly quoted material from a book or newspaper.

   a. Commas and periods are always placed inside the closing quotation marks.

      Our guide said, "Make your way to the back of the bus."

      "Make your way to the back of the bus," our guide said.

      Our guide said, "Make your way to the back of the bus," and then he helped the next person up the steps.

   b. Place colons and semicolons outside the closing quotation marks.

      Our guide said, "Make your way to the back of the bus": a remark we were to hear often.

      Our guide said, "Make your way to the back of the bus"; he wanted to fill it in an orderly fashion, I guess.

   c. Place exclamation points and question marks inside the quotation marks when they belong to the quoted material; outside, when they belong to the sentence as a whole.

      "Make your way to the back of the bus!" I thought as I got on for the umpteenth time.

      I was so tired of hearing, "Make your way to the back of the bus"!

      We asked, "Will the money be used for their benefit?"

      Did anyone ask, "Will the money be used for their benefit"?

  2. Use single quotation marks (the apostrophe on the typewriter) to

enclose a quotation within a quotation. When there is a third quotation within a second, enclose it within double quotation marks.

> Aunt Mary said, "The minister came in and he said, 'Well, Mary, I've come to tell you something. Your father is on his way here now.' " Aunt Mary said, "I thought, 'Why is Father coming so soon?' And he said, 'Your father asked me to give you a message before he got here: "I've married your dead mother's sister." ' "

3. Colloquial expressions and slang should not be placed in quotation marks. The following examples are *incorrect*.

> Our family was full of "kissing cousins." Everybody was drinking "white mule"—that was bootleg whiskey.

4. Inanimate objects cannot speak, even though we say they give us messages. Do not place such messages in quotation marks.

> The sign said No Trespassing.
> (Capital letters are used to give a sign-like appearance.)
> The man's clothes and car said money.
> (Note that no capital letters are used.)

5. Do not use quotation marks to enclose only approximations or summations of what another person said.

> When she said yes, we went ahead with our plans.
> The boss said do it that way, so we did it that way.

6. When a speaker says the word quote before relating someone else's words or before making a tongue-in-cheek comment, set the word quote off with commas or dashes, if commas would cause confusion, and use quotation marks around the words that follow it.

> It seemed to be that he was, quote, "too busy."
> People said that he wasn't able to—quote—"serve the congregation," that he wasn't well enough to do it.

IX. Spelling

A. Verify the spelling of the names of people, places, organizations; the titles of books; technical terms, jargon, and colloquialisms.

B. Words with more than one accepted spelling should be spelled in only one way throughout the transcript.

C. Common contractions used in writing should be typed and retained if they are verbatim. Do not invent contractions to try to convey dialect.

> that's, could've—but not—more'n'enuf, lots'a'time

D. Do not drop word endings and misspell insignificant mispronounced words to try to convey dialect.

> get—not—git   going—not—going'
> because—not—cuz   and—not—'n'

E. Compile an office reference list of words which are frequently misspelled, homonyms, and similarly pronounced words whose spellings and meanings are sometimes confused.

EDITING SYMBOLS

MEANING INTENDED	EXAMPLES
Capitalize	we moved to Atlantic city.
Set in lower case	We moved from Little Athens.
Underline	I read the New York Times.
Transpose words or letters	It was a (day/hot) but we worked on.
Use the other form—spell out, use figures, do or don't abbreviate	Of our (5) daughters, one is (twenty-one). We grow roses, daisies, glads, (etc.)
Delete—word, letter, punctuation	It was a hot, hot morning.
Leave in or let stand as originally	It was a hot, hot morning.
Leave a space	Walking is good exercise for all.
Close up the space	Let's do some thing special.
Start a new paragraph	The coat fit. We also bought food.
No new paragraph	We also bought food. The fruit was fresh and crisp.
Insert letters or words	Bring your car around to back.
Insert punctuation—other than dash, hyphen, period	He said, he called his mother's home."
Insert dash	The car the red one stopped.
Insert hyphen	Onehalf the usual amount is needed.
Insert period	The coat fit so, we left for home then.

Additional Sources

For background and technical information on oral history:

Baum, Willa. *Oral History for the Local Historical Society.* 2d ed., rev. Nashville, Tenn.: American Assn. for State and Local History, 1974.

Mason, Elizabeth B., and Starr, Louis M., eds. *The Oral History Collection of Columbia University.* New York: Oral History Research Office, 1973.

Moss, William W. *Oral History Program Manual.* New York: Praeger, 1974.

Shumway, Gary L., and Hartley, William G. *An Oral History Primer.* Fullerton, Calif.: California State Univ. Oral History Program, 1973.

Starr, Louis M. "Oral History: Problems and Prospects." In *Advances in Librarianship*, vol. 2, edited by Melvin J. Voigt, pp. 275–304. New York: Academic Pr., 1971.

Tyrell, William G. *Tape-Recording Local History.* Technical Leaflet 35. Nashville, Tenn.: American Assn. for State and Local History, 1966.

Useful bibliographies and guides to oral history programs:

Meckler, Alan, and McMullin, Ruth, eds. *Oral History Collections.* New York: Bowker, 1975.

Shumway, Gary. *Oral History in the United States: A Directory.* New York: Oral History Assn., 1971.

Waserman, Manfred J., ed. *Bibliography on Oral History.* 2d ed., rev. New York: Oral History Assn., 1975.

Basic reference books:

Skillin, Marjorie E., and Gay, Robert M. *Words into Type.* 3d ed., rev. Englewood Cliffs, N.J.: Prentice-Hall, Inc., 1974.

Turabian, Kate L. *A Manual for Writers of Term Papers, Theses, and Dissertations.* 4th ed., rev. Chicago: Univ. of Chicago Pr., 1973.

For general information on indexing and cataloging an oral history collection:

Atkins, Thomas V., ed. *Cross Reference Index: A Subject Heading Guide.* New York: Bowker, 1974.

Boll, John J. *Introduction to Cataloging.* Vols. 1 and II. New York: McGraw-Hill, 1970.

Collison, Robert L. *Indexes and Indexing.* 4th ed., rev. New York: DeGraff, 1969.

Needham, C. D. *Organizing Knowledge in Libraries: An Introduction to Information Retrieval.* New York: Academic Pr., 1971.

Westby, Barbara M., ed. *Sears List of Subject Headings.* 10th ed. New York: H. W. Wilson, 1972.

Selected books illustrating varied uses of oral history sources:

Broadfoot, Barry. *Ten Lost Years, 1929–1939: Memories of Canadians Who Survived the Depression.* Toronto: Doubleday Canada, 1973.

Bullock, Paul. *Watts: The Aftermath; An Inside View of the Ghetto.* New York: Grove Pr., 1969.

Burns, James MacGregor. *Roosevelt: Soldier of Freedom 1940–1945.* New York: Harcourt, 1970.

Frankfurter, Felix. *Felix Frankfurter Reminisces.* New York: Reynal, 1960.

Joseph, Peter. *Good Times: An Oral History of America in the Nineteen Sixties.* New York: William Morrow, 1974.

Hamburger, Robert. *Our Portion of Hell: Fayette County, Tennessee; An Oral History of the Struggle for Civil Rights.* New York: Links, 1973.

Miller, Merle. *Plain Speaking: An Oral Biography of Harry S. Truman.* New York: Berkley/Putnam, 1974.

Montell, William Lynwood. *The Saga of Coe Ridge: A Study in Oral History.* Knoxville: Univ. of Tennessee Pr., 1970.

Rosengarten, Theodore. *All God's Dangers: The Life of Nate Shaw.* New York: Knopf, 1974.

Terkel, Studs. *Hard Times: An Oral History of the Great Depression.* New York: Pantheon, 1970.

Williams, T. Harry. *Huey Long.* New York: Knopf, 1969.